UNDERCOVER INVESTIGATION
THIRD EDITION

UNDERCOVER
INVESTIGATION
THIRD EDITION

J. Kirk Barefoot

Butterworth–Heinemann

Boston • Oxford • Melbourne • Singapore • Toronto • Munich • New Delhi • Tokyo

Library of Congress Cataloging-in-Publication Data

Barefoot, J. Kirk.
Undercover investigation / by J. Kirk Barefoot —3rd ed.
  p. cm.
  Includes bibliographical references and index.
  ISBN 0-7506-9645-1 (hardcover)
  1. Undercover operations. I. Title.
HV8080.U5B37 1995
363.2'32—dc20   95-38
                                                            CIP

British Library Cataloguing-in-Publication Data
A catalogue record for this book is available from the British Library.

The publisher offers discounts on bulk orders of this book.
For information, please write:

Manager of Special Sales
Butterworth–Heinemann
313 Washington Street
Newton, MA 02158-1626

10 9 8 7 6 5 4 3 2 1

Printed in the United States of America

Contents

Foreword   vii
Preface   ix
Acknowledgments   xi
Introduction   xiii
About the Author   xv

1. Brief History of Undercover Work   1
2. Recruiting and Selecting Undercover Personnel   13
3. Training   19
4. The Cover   47
5. The Assignment   61
6. Roping   71
7. Entrapment and Testimony   89
8. Supervision and Communications   99
9. The Burn   109
10. Shopping Investigations and Surveillance   115

Conclusion   135
Bibliography   137
Index   139

Foreword

This book by J. Kirk Barefoot is *sui generis* (one of a kind): a slim volume, yet one capable of fully informing or training readers on undercover investigations. The publication of this third edition is proof of the directness of Barefoot's approach to teaching undercover investigations. At John Jay College of Criminal Justice, I have seen its revelatory effects on scores—perhaps hundreds—of students who have profited from earlier editions.

What is it about Barefoot's concepts that gives them such appeal? For one thing, the author's positive attitude toward undercover operations permeates each chapter. He is passionately convinced that undercover skills are learnable. He believes that with diligence and proper training, most people who are interested in the craft can become competent investigators and that those few, rare people with exceptional ability at "roping" can, with further training and support, hone their skills and become exceptional undercover agents. From that premise, Barefoot provides the essence of the training, just as he has done at periodic undercover schools that he and others have conducted over the years.

Another aspect of this book is its sheer persuasiveness. Barefoot believes that many private industry and public police managers are too timid at establishing or vigorously expanding undercover programs when such strategy clearly beckons. Perhaps they feel that it is too costly, or illegal, or too bewilderingly complex for them to manage, that such investigations belong on the multiplex screen but not at their workplace. Other managers fail to perceive that the huge costs of systematic losses can only be resolved through this type of confidential internal probe. Such reticence will be dissolved by the following pages, in which case histories repeatedly empha-size the cost benefits, legal status, and simplicity of managing an undercover operative program. The author is directing his manu-script to newcomers to the field of undercover work, but one feels that it is equally aimed at the old-timers who allow problems to fes-ter that a well-conceived undercover program would identify and eradicate.

A final quality that, I believe, makes this book strong is its underlying moral premise. No sermon is contained herein, but Barefoot feels deeply that employees and their accomplices who systematically put at risk, vandalize, or steal from their workplaces should be identified for the sake of the organization, for society as a whole, and for the perpetrators' own long-term benefits. Such malefactors put jobs at risk and bleed the profits and spirit from an organization. As Barefoot makes clear, undercover efforts also aid law enforcement agencies in stamping out the criminal activity that normally exceeds the capacity of overt investigations. A suc-cessfully concluded undercover operation delivers practical and personal satisfaction to those involved at all levels.

In this edition, Barefoot introduces considerable new mate-rial on such topics as establishing the cover; sequencing assign-ments for the undercover agent; roping in the dishonest; and catching thieves and others without incurring legal liability. Other new chapters help the undercover manager operate more effec-tively, reminding him or her to use the communications that were not so readily available when earlier editions of this book were published.

This volume emphasizes the art and practice of undercover operations. It demystifies a management strategy that is too fre-quently misunderstood and too rarely employed.

Robert D. McCrie
Professor, John Jay College of Criminal Justice, the City University of New York, and editor, *Security Letter* and *Security Journal*

Preface

The objective of this text is to provide the security administrator or law enforcement official with guidelines for establishing an undercover operation. More important, it is hoped that the book will serve as a training manual for new undercover agents and as a refresher for experienced agents.

The need for such a text is evident. There is a dearth of published material on undercover work, and the publications that do exist on this subject deal almost exclusively with short-term undercover assignments, such as those used to make "buys" of narcotics, counterfeit money, or other contraband. The techniques involved in this kind of activity are not designed for the long-term infiltration of a criminal gang. Cover stories are designed to withstand only a cursory inspection—certainly not the intense scrutiny that one must expect in a long-term assignment.

Since the publication of the first edition of this text, many investigative agencies have expanded their training programs for prospective undercover agents. We have also seen a general recognition of the importance of accurate report writing and a new understanding of entrapment on the part of agents. Labor arbitrators and many judges have become even stricter in their interpretation of the fine line between roping and entrapment. For this reason, the chapters on these issues have been expanded and updated in this edition.

Acknowledgments

Harry S. Lindberg, retired regional security manager for Mc-Kesson Corporation, was to have been a coauthor of this book. For personal reasons, he was forced to withdraw during the discussion phase. Nevertheless, I am deeply indebted to Mr. Lindberg for his many ideas and suggestions, which I have incorporated into this book. Mr. Lindberg was the agent involved in many of the case studies described in this book, and consequently, he is responsible for many of the philosophies and concepts of undercover work presented herein.

Finally, I must acknowledge the late Dr. V.A. Leonard, former professor emeritus of Washington State University and author of the foreword to the first and second editions of this book. It was Dr. Leonard who first proposed the idea for the book and who encouraged its beginning.

Introduction

The year 1973 was notable for the security industry because of the United States Supreme Court's decision in the *Weingarten* case. The impact of this decision on private security is similar to that of the *Miranda* decision on law enforcement agencies, in that members of bargaining units are now entitled to representation during an interrogation if they request it. This would be similar to the police interrogating a suspect in the presence of his attorney.

During the fifties and sixties, it was common practice for security executives to rely on their interrogation skills, possibly supplemented by polygraph examinations, to break suspected larceny cases. A security official of a large mail-order house in Chicago, for example, regularly strolled the order-filling and packing departments, looking over the employees as they went about their tasks. Using that "sixth sense" that is unique to many security practitioners, he would settle on a particular employee who did not look right to him. After summoning the suspected employee to the security office, he began an interrogation that more often than not resulted in the employee's confession of the theft of company property. Needless to say, there was never any evidence of wrongdoing beforehand, and the whole procedure amounted to little more than a fishing expedition.

In those days, even though the work force was organized by a labor union, the security chief was under no obligation to provide union representation during the interrogation. In fact, the labor laws of the time clearly stated that union representation was not necessary during the investigation; a representative need only be present during disciplinary action.

All of this changed when the Supreme Court mandated union representation for members of bargaining units if they requested it during interrogation, in *National Labor Relations Board v. J. Weingarten, Inc.* (1973). As a result of the *Weingarten* decision, old-fashioned investigative work is necessary before the interrogation of suspected union members. In other words, the security executive should have enough of a case before the interrogation to be able to take disciplinary action against the suspect and discharge him or her based on evidence already developed. This brings the pendulum back to one of the basic investigative tools, namely, undercover.

About the Author

J. Kirk Barefoot, C.P.P., is a retired director of risk management for Cluett, Peabody & Company, a multifacility apparel manufacturing and retailing company headquartered in New York City. After his retirement, Mr. Barefoot was president of Cluett Security Services, later known as J. Kirk Barefoot and Associates. Before joining Cluett, Peabody & Company, he was director of security for McKesson Corporation, a San Francisco–based wholesale drug firm. Mr. Barefoot now serves as a consultant to U.S. industry. He is frequently called on to give expert testimony in court cases involving undercover investigations.

The author's interest in the security field and undercover operations in particular was kindled when he worked with a military intelligence team in the Philippines. Headed by famed army insurgency experts Colonel Wendell Fertig and Major Joseph Rice, the group operated undercover in central Luzon, evaluating the strength and potential of the Communist-led Hukbalhap (Huks). Following this service with Army intelligence, Mr. Barefoot earned a B.S. in police science and administration at Washington State University.

A frequent speaker and lecturer on the subjects of internal theft investigation and undercover operations, Mr. Barefoot is the author of *Employee Theft Investigation* (1990) and co-author of *Corporate Security Administration and Management* (1987) and is the editor and principal author of *The Polygraph Story* (1974).

Mr. Barefoot is a life member and past president of the American Polygraph Association. He is a life member of the American Society for Industrial Security and formerly served on its board of directors.

Brief History of Undercover Work

Undercover work, as we know it today, probably had its origin in military campaigns. In U.S. history, we can find examples of military intelligence operatives as far back as the American Revolution. The colonies benefited from the talents of the great patriot, Nathan Hale, and the British had a spy of their own, John André. From the Civil War period, the accomplishments of Belle Boyd for the South and Allan Pinkerton[1] for the North must be recognized. World War I cannot be reviewed without mentioning the infamous Mata Hari. In World War II, more sophisticated intelligence-gathering and undercover methods were employed. The activities of the American Office of Strategic Services must be recognized. This organization was the forerunner of our present-day C.I.A.

The Cold War era brought into focus the activities of such people as Russian Colonel Rudolph Abel and Matthew Cevetic.[2] Abel was probably the highest ranking and most successful spy who ever infiltrated the United States. Cevetic, a famous undercover agent of the Federal Bureau of Investigation (FBI), infiltrated the Communist party. The Cold War also focused attention on the seldom acknowledged but often speculated-about activities of the Central Intelligence Agency (CIA).

The basic difference between the work of these people and that of present-day undercover agents is one of semantics. Military operatives are called *spies*—a word that sometimes connotes unsavory business. In industrial security and law enforcement, we have attempted to give some measure of respectability to intelligence gatherers by calling them *undercover agents* or *undercover operatives*. Regardless of the terms used, the game is basically the same: deep penetration of and gathering of information about the opposition.

LAW ENFORCEMENT

Law enforcement agencies have used undercover techniques to varying degrees in the past. One of the earliest uses was the infiltration of train robbery gangs by Pinkerton agents following the Civil War. In recent years, the public has become aware, through the media, of undercover operations that arose from unique situations. For example, crime commissions sometimes recruit an experienced investigator from another city to work undercover to infiltrate a suspected allegiance between local politicians and organized crime.

The more progressive police departments, such as those in Los Angeles, Chicago, and New York, have long maintained intelligence units with the sole responsibility of gathering information concerning local organized crime. Much of the information developed by these units has resulted from the efforts of undercover police officers.

Although a less formalized practice, most city police departments have for many years assigned rookie patrol officers to work undercover in the vice division. Members of organized crime, local gambling operators, and prostitutes make it their business to get to know the faces of as many members of the police department as possible. For this reason, rookie officers are always in demand for undercover assignments in the vice and narcotics units.

Some of the longer term undercover activities of local law enforcement have come into sharp focus recently because of the need for police agencies to infiltrate radical organizations that are dedicated to violence, disruption of law and order, or the overthrow of government processes. In the Black Panther trials in New York, for example, the undercover assignments by the New York City Police Department ran several years.

Police undercover operations in the late seventies were often described by the media as *sting* operations. In these operations, the local or state police took over a vacant storefront or warehouse and posed as professional fences (buyers of stolen goods). Over a period of many months, the undercover officers purchased large amounts of contraband from thieves and other criminals. The business grew by word of mouth, encouraging repeat visits by criminals. When the police officers had gathered enough physical and other evidence, they sprang the trap and rounded up all of the criminals with whom they had done business. Sting operations were conducted in many cities across the United States and seemed to be in vogue for a time. No doubt today, the criminal population is extremely wary of dealing with fences who lack the proper credentials.

MILITARY AND FEDERAL INTELLIGENCE AGENCIES

The major military services have always given intelligence gathering a top priority. Intelligence gathering in the U.S. Navy falls under the office of the Naval Investigations Services Organization (NISO). In the air force, it is included in the activities of the Office of Special Investigations (OSI), and in the army, it has usually been a function of the G-2 Section. Although actual undercover operations are probably more commonplace in the army than in the other branches, all military services have engaged in undercover operations at one time or another. To combat or counter the activities of other nations' undercover agents, the U.S. Army has developed a unit called the Counter Intelligence Corps. Both the navy and the air force have people engaged in comparable activity.

The biggest civilian-operated intelligence-gathering unit today is the CIA. Unlike its sister agencies—the National Security Agency (NSA) and the Army Security Agency (ASA)—the CIA engages in many undercover activities throughout the world. Although new techologies have led to the introduction of sophisticated electronic products to aid in intelligence gathering, there is still no substitute for the work of the undercover agent.

The number one domestic antiespionage agency in the United States is the FBI. Unlike many other federal agencies, the FBI relies more on finding paid informants and recruiting from outside the ranks than on assigning its own special agents to work undercover. Examples of successful undercover operatives who were recruited by the FBI from the outside are Matthew Cevetic and Herbert A. Philbrick.[3]

One example of law enforcement's use of undercover methods is the so-called Abscam operation of the early eighties. As a result of these undercover efforts, the FBI was able to obtain successful prosecutions of a number of government figures, including members of Congress, and several private attorneys. The key undercover operative in each of these cases was identified as the government's chief informant, Mel Weinberg. A close study of the Abscam cases reveals that their success hinged on Weinberg's ability to "rope" the suspects. (See Chapter 6.) Defense attorneys maintained that Weinberg's efforts at roping constituted entrapment, but the government successfully overcame this contention in the trials. In the legal sense, then, entrapment did not play a major role in these investigative efforts.

A more recent use of undercover methods was revealed in the aftermath of the World Trade Center bombing in New York City. In this case, the FBI used a former Egyptian intelligence officer, Emad Eldin Aly Abdou Salem, to infiltrate a ring of Arab terrorists. Emad Salem's efforts were so productive that an even larger conspiracy involving the infamous Arab cleric, Sheik Omar Abdel-Rahman, was uncovered to blow up major points in New York City and to assassinate certain political figures.

The federal law enforcement agency that is held in highest esteem for its undercover accomplishments is the old Federal Bureau of Narcotics.[4] This agency's expertise in undercover work resulted from the very nature of the cases that it handled, rather than from any particular leaning toward this type of investigative approach. Today's undercover narcotics agents are frequently loaned to other federal law enforcement agencies. The average Treasury, Secret Service, or FBI agent runs to a definite type and often does not have the proper mental attitude or physical appearance to be successful in infiltrating an underworld gang. Many narcotic and drug agents, on the other hand, seem to be selected for their physical appearance, which lends itself to successful undercover work. As an example, one of my undercover agents had the classic appearance of a drug addict. He eventually accepted a position with the Federal Bureau of Narcotics and became a very successful undercover agent for that agency.

BUSINESS AND INDUSTRY

You might be surprised to learn that, outside of government service, the vast majority of undercover agents are found in business and industry, not law enforcement. Some of these undercover agents are employed directly by corporations for internal investigation, but most are employed by private agencies that contract with businesses to provide investigative services.

The number of undercover operatives working in business and industry reflects the devastating impact of crime on U.S. companies. It is difficult to arrive at an accurate cost of this crime for two reasons. First, many companies are reluctant to file fidelity claims with their insurance carriers because frequent claims ultimately result in higher insurance premiums. Most companies use their fidelity insurance only in the case of a defalcation that would amount to corporate disaster. Second, many thefts in business and industry are not reported simply because they are never discovered.

No current estimates are available of the cost of employee theft to U.S. business and industry. However, the FBI's Financial

Institution Fraud and Failure (FIF) statistics, reported in the March 1, 1992, edition of *Security Letter*, point in the right direction. The FBI's figures show a reported loss of $606,154,000 in 1986, rising to $2,280,551,000 in 1991, an increase of 26.5 percent. Economic analysts conclude that the increase was due mostly to greed and self-interest.

The National Retail Federation, a trade group, reports that in 1992, U.S. retailers reported $27 billion in shortages. The group estimates that of this number, $11 billion was due to employee theft. Based on all available data, employee theft is still running at gigantic proportions. However, the rate of growth has undoubtedly been slowed by the new philosophies and loss prevention techniques practiced by professionals in the American Society for Industrial Security.

Impact of Undercover Investigations

To understand the impact that undercover investigations can have on a corporation's profit picture, let's look at the history of McKesson Corporation, which began an undercover program in the late fifties. McKesson (formerly McKesson & Robbins, Inc.) is the largest wholesale distributor of drugstore products. Sales now exceed $12 billion per year.

At a company conference in December 1959, officials of McKesson Corporation estimated the cost of losses due to internal theft at more than $1 million per year. After a series of successful undercover cases over the next six years, officials of the company acknowledged that internal theft had been reduced to about $250,000 annually on a sales volume that had increased to $1 billion per year.

Private Agencies and Company Undercover Agents

Because of the cost of theft to U.S. business and industry today, the undercover departments of the old-line private detective agencies are flourishing. New agencies specializing in undercover work have sprung up and are enjoying a sizable portion of the undercover business.

As mentioned earlier, most industrial undercover operatives are employed either by agencies specializing in undercover work or by private detective agencies. Some of the more prominent nationwide agencies specializing in undercover investigations include Management Safeguards; Investigation, Inc.; and Lincoln Controls, all of which are headquartered in New York. Three of the largest private detective agencies that operate undercover departments are Burns Security Services, Parsippany, New Jersey; Pinkerton Detective Agency, Inc., Los Angeles, California; and Wackenhut Agency, Coral Gables, Florida.

There are, of course, other very competent organizations that offer undercover service. Often, a strictly local agency is better suited to a particular job than is an organization that operates nationwide. The mark of quality in industrial undercover work is the ability of the undercover operatives themselves and the quality of their supervision. These two factors determine the success of the investigation.

In recent years, a number of large companies have developed their own undercover investigative staff. Before embarking on such a venture, a number of factors must be considered. A company working on a do-it-yourself basis cannot compete with a private agency in terms of the diversity and flexibility of personnel. Does the position call for an accountant, an engineer, a teacher, a pilot, or some other professional person? If so, most agencies have qualified people on tap or can recruit the necessary help. Agencies are also able to make substitutions of personnel when the need arises, as it occasionally does. Other advantages of using an agency include better training and supervision. If a company lacks personnel with the professional skill necessary for training and supervision, it would be disastrous to attempt in-house undercover efforts.

With all of the advantages of using an outside agency, why would a company even consider developing its own undercover staff? The first and most important answer is financial. For a four-week job where the worker's salary is $200 per week, an agency might charge $1,500 or more over and above the ordinary wages paid to the operative, resulting in a four-week cost of $2,300. On a do-it-yourself basis, the same four weeks' work might cost about $2,000. The agent is presumed to be carried on a corporate payroll, and the local wages earned ($800) are deducted monthly from the corporate salary, leaving a net cost of $1,200 for a four-week effort. Of course, a company does not get off quite this easily. To this must be added the costs of moving from one city to another, plus salary and expenses while engaged in setting up a proper cover (Table 1.1).

Many companies over the years have tried agency personnel and become so dissatisfied as to sour on the whole concept of un-

Table 1.1 Comparative Costs of In-house and Agency Undercover Work

Item	In-house	Agency	Remarks
Base salary (monthly)	$2,000	$1,500	Agency charge to client
Local salary	−800	+800	
Net	1,200	2,300	Base outlay by company
Incidental expenses (monthly)	60	60	
Subtotal	1,260	2,360	
Living subsidy	None	100	If from out of town
Subtotal	1,260	2,460	
Relocation expense, maximum (prorated monthly based on two relocates per year)	250	75	If from out of town
Subtotal	1,510	2,535	
Cover expense (prorated)	75	40	
Total	1,585	2,575	May be minimum only

dercover. In all fairness, however, not all the blame can be laid at the agency's doorstep. This is illustrated by the experience of McKesson Corporation.

When the McKesson security department was formed in 1954, it was headed by a retired Secret Service agent, Frank Seckler. Seckler had spent most of his twenty or so years with the government doing undercover work—not only for the Secret Service, but also on loan to other Treasury enforcement agencies. He had become the most famous and successful undercover agent in the history of the U.S. government, and his exploits were serialized by newspaper chains upon his retirement. Without question, he knew the business as no one else did.

After joining McKesson, Seckler tried to infiltrate suspected company theft rings by hiring agency personnel. In most cases, the results were unsatisfactory, and the agency's services were terminated. When the author was appointed director of security at the company in 1958 after Seckler's death, these failures were studied to determine their cause. Here's what was found:

1. Seckler himself was a highly trained perfectionist, and agency personnel did not measure up to his own abilities.
2. Agency costs were high, even in the mid-fifties. As a wholesaler, McKesson was extremely cost-conscious, and this was the source of pressure to obtain results within 30 days.
3. The company's new security controls worked against the undercover operation and completely ruled out the possibility of an early break within 30 days.
4. Most agency personnel did not take a personal interest in the case. For some, it was just another in a long series of assignments.
5. Many agency operatives were on their first case and had received only a minimum of training and orientation. They were given printed instructions on what to look for and what to report. They had no coaching on the art of roping. In some cases, their reports were given verbally to an agency "rewrite person" who composed the report for the day.

Based on these findings, a new plan was submitted to top management—one that was to prove practical in case after case. It was a new concept in undercover work: company undercover operatives.

Management had to be educated about this new concept of long-term undercover investigation. No longer would the company move against an individual thief exposed in the first 30 days or so of the undercover investigation. Internal theft in a company is like a cancer. Every vestige must be exposed during an investigation so that the cancer can be eliminated or controlled. To apprehend only several thieves among dozens does not cure the problem. At best, it leads to only a temporary deterrent effect, following which the thieves become more sophisticated and cautious in their activities. Furthermore, the techniques used by security managers in both the undercover phase and the "bust" phase might be a one-shot effort, just as the cancer surgeon might only be given one opportunity at major and radical surgery.

Experience has shown that the average industrial undercover case lasts six months. In most instances, it takes three months for the agent to gain the full acceptance of the other workers. The remaining three months are devoted to building a case that will stand up and that will give interrogators an overwhelming advantage over the suspects during the bust.

NOTES

1. After the Civil War, Allan Pinkerton and his family played a large part in the settling of the western states by providing security for the federal government and for the railroads. The outgrowth of this activity was the founding of the Pinkerton Detective Agency, which is one of the largest of the national private agencies. The agency has continued its tradition of intelligence gathering and today offers undercover service to many industrial clients throughout the United States.
2. During the forties, Cevetic was recruited and coached by the FBI to infiltrate the Communist party in the Pittsburgh, Pennsylvania, district. As a result of his undercover work,

leaders of the party were prosecuted by the State of Pennsylvania in what was probably the only sedition trial ever conducted by a state. Cevetic's exploits are well documented in his book, *The Big Decision* (1959).

3. Like Cevetic, Philbrick was an undercover agent who successfully infiltrated the Communist party in the United States. His exploits were documented in a television series entitled "I Led Three Lives."

4. The Federal Bureau of Narcotics, formerly a part of the United States Treasury Department, was merged with the Bureau of Drug Abuse Control (BDAC) in 1968. The new agency, which falls under the jurisdiction of the Justice Department, is now known as the Drug Enforcement Administration (DEA).

2

Recruiting and Selecting Undercover Personnel

RECRUITING UNDERCOVER PERSONNEL

The success of any business endeavor depends heavily on the people who make up that business. Without quality people no company or business can succeed in the long run. The investigative business, including undercover operations, is no different. Not every investigator is capable of doing good undercover work, and, in fact, the majority of detectives and investigators are not. It requires a special type of person and one who must be matched to the job assignment. Thus, recruiting and selection are major factors in this highly specialized field.

Local Law Enforcement

In large urban police departments, the problem of recruiting undercover officers is usually easily resolved. Police departments in large metropolitan centers like New York, Chicago, and Los Angeles generally have no difficulty selecting appropriate undercover officers. They can take their pick from the various ethnic and racial backgrounds represented by the graduating class of the local police academy. Many rookie patrol officers look forward to undercover assignments with the narcotics division or the vice squad. Unlike these short-term undercover jobs, the more hazardous, long-term undercover assignments involved in subversive infiltration more properly call for volunteers.

Because of their size in numbers and geographical coverage, with proper labor planning, the availability of undercover officers from within state police organizations should be entirely practical. Although not necessarily larger in terms of total personnel, state police organizations have one advantage over local law enforcement agencies: they operate statewide. Thus, they can bring to a troubled area trained undercover officers from other parts of the state.

For small to medium-size city police departments and for local sheriff's offices, the main problems are the department's narrow geographic jurisdiction and limited personnel. The only obvious solution for smaller departments, which could normally engage only in the briefest of undercover assignments, is to provide sufficient funds in the budget to hire outside undercover services. Competent undercover officers might be obtained on loan from the state police or from another local department.

If this is impossible, the local department might contract with a private agency for the specific undercover type needed. As mentioned in the preceding chapter, private agencies have a definite advantage in being able to supply the exact type of individual required for a specific assignment. Sometimes, the personnel available from a private agency would obviously not be physically able to meet basic police qualifications. Obvious differences in size and outward appearance automatically lend the agents some degree of immunity to suspicion.

Private Agencies

Surprisingly enough, most undercover operatives employed by private agencies are recruited through newspaper advertisements.

Naturally, private agencies prefer undercover operatives with prior experience, but these men and women are difficult to find. Agencies are often forced to hire individuals without prior investigative training, which the agency must provide.

With the exception of some technicians or specialists, few operatives have had college or university training. Those who have had formal educational training beyond high school are not kept on undercover assignments for more than a year or so. They invariably end up in supervisory positions within the undercover department or are transferred to management training programs in other departments.

At best, most undercover personnel employed by agencies have a high school education. Many operatives are not even high school graduates. They have built-in deficiencies that their supervisors must recognize and handle. However, a surprising number of poorly educated operatives are extremely adept at the art of roping. In contrast, many with more formal education find the art of roping extremely difficult to master. In their undercover assignments, they are forced to rely on their powers of observation and deductive reasoning.

In-house Security Departments

Many companies that have attempted undercover operations on their own have employed the same basic recruiting techniques that private agencies use. That is, they attempt to employ undercover operatives with prior experience. Few of the companies recruiting in this manner have any sort of comprehensive training program, and they are dependent on experienced operatives. The recruitment of experienced operatives is the only sensible route for smaller companies.

On the other hand, some national corporations with security departments have tried to recruit their undercover staffs from colleges and universities that offer two- and four-year programs in criminal justice, law enforcement, or industrial security. For example, McKesson Corporation recruited undercover investigators from Michigan State University, Washington State University, and many others. In all, dozens of colleges and universities offer either two- or four-year programs in law enforcement subjects. Corporate security executives are often able to attract graduating seniors who, because of physical limitations like height, weight, and eyesight, would not be accepted by local or federal law enforcement agencies.

The following list illustrates some of the common differences between young people who are fresh out of criminal justice programs and experienced operatives from the street.

Criminal Justice Graduate	**Experienced Operative**
Poor at roping	Good at roping (see below)
Familiar with legalities of work	Does not know legalities of work
Can write acceptable reports	Poor report writer; needs rewrite person
Comes across as professional on the witness stand	Makes poor to fair impression in court
Does not blend in; is "straight"	Blends in; is streetwise

These comparisons are certainly not meant to be absolute, but they are based on common observations. Most deficiencies can be corrected through adequate training. Even the lack of formal college education can be offset by training and experience.

By offering career opportunities in security, corporations can often attract graduating college seniors who prove to be valuable additions to the security operation. A proper on-the-job training program with periodic promotion must be laid out in advance. The typical graduating senior is either single or newly married and thus can offer four to five years of periodic undercover work. Later, when there are children of school age in the family, the security executive must be prepared to reassign the undercover investigator to a more permanent and stable security position.

By interspersing undercover assignments with other investigative assignments like tail jobs, surveillance, and background and street-type investigations, the security executive keeps the monotony and boredom of undercover assignments to a minimum. This approach not only maintains the morale of college-trained undercover agents, but also gives them valuable experience in other areas of the security field in preparation for the day when they can leave undercover work for an open security assignment.

A word of caution is in order: Because of their family backgrounds and upbringing, many criminal justice students are never able to adapt successfully to undercover work. They find the art of roping difficult, if not impossible, to master. Selective security recruiters attempt to recruit potential undercover agents with a middle- or lower-class background. They look for candidates who have had some job experience, perhaps as a truck driver, laborer, dock worker, stock clerk, or janitor. The more education a candidate has had in the "school of hard knocks," the better his or her chances of success as an undercover agent. Another major drawback in recruiting from criminal justice programs is the scarcity of students from minority backgrounds. Competition for these students is very keen, and the corporate executive who lands minority graduates is fortunate.

Finally, the corporate executive should not overlook the possibility of recruiting undercover operatives from the ranks of present employees. Although this method is not generally recommended, it has sometimes proved successful and might be the only answer to infiltration.

SELECTING UNDERCOVER PERSONNEL

In addition to normal personnel screening devices, such as a physical examination and an IQ test, there are two tests of great importance for screening undercover candidates. The first is a questionnaire designed to evaluate the candidate's psychological profile. Undercover agents must be free of any psychological abnormalities that might interfere with a successful undercover operation, including severe anxieties, excessive irritability, and evasiveness.

The second important screening tool is a test of retentive powers (memory). Many undercover investigations are built around a collection of minute and seemingly insignificant facts, and the investigator is usually unable to take notes on the spot. For this reason, an unusual memory that is particularly attuned to names, faces, identifying marks, description, and so forth is a practical necessity. There is at least one good written test available to measure memory.[1]

The most critical test for an undercover candidate—a polygraph examination—is no longer available to private employers. Effective December 1988, the federal government prohibited the use of virtually all preemployment and periodic polygraph tests for private industry. (Governmental employers are exempted and can still use polygraph tests to screen job applicants.) For private employers, the only remedy to this dilemma is the use of a good paper-and-pencil test for honesty. There are a number of effective tests on the market, including the original one, the Reid Report, which has undergone about 20 revisions since its introduction.[2]

NOTES

1. Memory Test, Industrial Psychology, Inc., 111 N. Market St., Chicago, IL 61820.
2. Developed by John E. Reid & Associates, the test, which is now accepted by the scientific community, is marketed by Reid Psychological Systems, 200 S. Michigan, Chicago, IL 60604.

Training

3

Having selected and recruited promising undercover candidates, the investigations executive must now provide an adequate basic training program. To not do so almost ensures the ultimate failure of the program. The basic training should be designed to accomplish as an absolute minimum the changing of the student's thought process to that of an undercover agent's. It is the author's opinion that "advanced" training comes with on-the-job experience coupled with proper debriefings and coaching by the agent's handler.

PRIVATE AGENCIES

The problem of training, or rather the lack of it, is probably the largest single factor retarding the growth of the industrial undercover services offered by private agencies. Many corporate executives have said, "We tried undercover once, and I'd never do it again." There are probably many reasons for this sentiment, but all can be traced back to a common cause: the lack of formal training given to new undercover operatives before their assignment.

Table 3.1   Use of Undercover Agents by Companies (%)

	Size of Company		
	Small	Large	All
Never	76	51	62
Rarely	13	25	20
Periodically	9	12	11
Often	1	3	2
No response	1	9	5

Three-fourths of small companies and one-half of large companies have never used an undercover agent (Table 3.1). Among large companies, undercover agents are used either "periodically" or "often" by 15 percent of the firms (private survey conducted in 1987 by J. Kirk Barefoot & Associates, New York, NY). Without question, if all agencies could offer adequately trained undercover agents to business and industry, the use of such services by corporations would increase by at least 50 percent.

This is not to say that all industrial undercover personnel employed by agencies are incompetent because of their lack of training. Many have developed into highly competent agents simply by using good judgment and making the most of their experiences over the years. They would do justice to any security organization fortunate enough to have them on the payroll. Unfortunately, not all undercover agents are this competent.

The rate of turnover in most agencies is quite high, and it is unusual to find many agents on a particular staff with as many as 10 years of service. In fact, it is quite common to encounter undercover agents working on their first (and possibly last) assignment. The basic philosophy of most security agencies is that the payroll costs for security personnel, including undercover operatives, guards, and investigators, should be billed to the client. Most agencies are reluctant to carry an employee on the payroll for training, standby work, and so on. One of the problems contributing to high turnover is that many agencies lay off undercover operatives at the conclusion of an assignment if a new assignment is not readily available. For this reason, the average undercover agent simply goes from one agency to another. Good agents are not retained on one particular payroll, and incompetent agents are able to perpetuate themselves in the industry for years.

When the author wrote the first edition of this text in the early seventies, he interviewed a number of undercover operatives from various agencies regarding their training. At the time, most training appeared to be minimal or almost nonexistent, except for a typewritten sheet of instructions about what to put in a report. This situation has changed for the better in the past 25 years. Many agencies have formalized their training of undercover recruits. At least one company, Management Safeguards, has prepared training sessions on videotape cassettes. A few agencies have lengthened the training period to five days.

Unfortunately, many of the smaller local agencies have not improved their training programs, and the industry is still plagued with ill-trained undercover operatives. Therefore, it is imperative that agency clients examine the training program while personally interviewing prospective agents.

Without adequate training, industrial undercover agents have little or no knowledge of the more important concepts of the work. They do not know how to recognize, mark, and preserve physical evidence of gambling, drugs, merchandise thefts, and so forth. Through experience and instinct, they might be adept at the art of roping, but they often know little or nothing about the rules of entrapment. Their court testimony is usually woeful compared to that of law enforcement professionals, and they present an inviting target to aggressive defense attorneys during cross-examination.

IN-HOUSE SECURITY DEPARTMENTS

It is because of these weaknesses in the industry that many companies have turned their energies toward developing their own undercover staff. At McKesson Corporation, for example, the development of an in-house staff and the best possible training led to success where private agencies had failed. In this section, the McKesson training program is examined in some detail in the hope that it will assist agencies and corporations in training of their own undercover agents.

Model Training Program

The undercover training program used at McKesson in the early sixties was established for in-house use only. In the early seventies, the program, which had proved quite successful, was sponsored jointly by McKesson and Cluett, Peabody & Company. The training program was improved with the production of videotapes on drug abuse, roping, and the "burn." Case material was edited to lighten the students' reading burden but still retain the essential lessons to be learned.

In 1979, Cluett and McKesson agreed to open the training program on a nonprofit, break-even basis to other companies that wished to participate. Later, personnel from security agencies as well as private corporations took part in the training program. In 1984, the school was administered by Cluett Security Service, a wholly owned subsidiary of Cluett, Peabody & Company. In 1987, Cluett Security Services became known as J. Kirk Barefoot & Associates, a division of Winfield Security Corporation of New York.

The training program consisted of approximately five days of instruction, including formal classroom lectures, outside reading assignments, and one-to-one coaching. The program's objective was not to develop experienced undercover agents in five days; rather, the goal was to teach the raw recruits to think like undercover agents and to give them resources to fall back on in the years ahead. For undercover agents with some experience in the field but no formal training, the program served as a finishing school to hone requisite skills. The school's philosophy acknowledged that experience in the field is the ultimate teacher.

The location of the school was flexible; it had been held in moderately priced hotels in Chicago, Atlanta, and Stamford, Connecticut.

The typical student was a recent graduate from an industrial security program or a four-year criminal justice program. A few students were not college graduates, but were recruited by their new employer because of their special skills. A few security executives audited the course to assist them in supervising their new undercover recruits. Several agency executives also participated with the intention of setting up their own commercial undercover schools.

Because of the nature of one-on-one training, each class was generally limited to 10 students, not counting auditors, and was taught by two instructors. A third instructor was available for assisting with classes that exceeded 10 students, but the maximum class size was set at 15.

Outline of Schedule

The students are assembled on Sunday evening for a get-acquainted session and an orientation to the upcoming week. Although the students get to know each other quite well during the week, a number of companies specifically request that their company affiliation not be revealed so as not to jeopardize the future cover stories of their agents. The instructors reinforce the importance of this precaution throughout the week, beginning with the opening session on Sunday evening.

Students are given hand-out material to orient them to specialty topics, such as organized gambling, and a copy of this book, which is used as a textbook for the course. These training materials become the students' personal property upon completion of the course.

The first part of a commercially prepared movie on undercover training is shown on Sunday evening, and the students are given specific reading assignments in the textbook to prepare them for the first day's lecture. This instruction technique—advance reading assignments in preparation for the following day's lecture—is used throughout the week.

In addition to the textbook, students are required to read at least six of nine general investigation cases that have been carefully selected and edited. There are sufficient copies of each case so that students need not wait for a copy and the faster readers are not hampered by the slower readers. In addition to the general investigation cases, students are also required to read one labor arbitration case involving major dishonesty, one federal circuit court of appeals decision on entrapment, and selected passages of *The Big Decision* (Cevetic, 1959).

Students are required to take notes on their readings so that they can discuss the cases intelligently with an instructor. In the general investigation cases, students are encouraged to place themselves mentally in the role of the original agent who wrote the report. They are encouraged to commend the agent, offer constructive criticisms, or criticize the agent's failures, as appropriate. A summary and teaching guide have been prepared for each of the general investigation cases so that the trainer can determine whether the student has understood the important points of the case.

Most of the afternoons and evenings during the week are taken up with these special reading assignments. The first morning may be generally devoted to specific classroom lectures covering such diverse subjects as these:

- History of undercover
- Handling of travel expense reports
- Handling of outside money earned at various jobs
- Claiming reimbursement for working overtime

Students are also lectured on how to establish local credit and how to submit medical claims and handle moving expenses so as not to jeopardize their cover stories.

On the second day, one lecture focuses on report writing, including both the appropriate format and frequency. This lecture is supplemented by a practical exercise in which the students are sent out of the hotel on diverse assignments, then asked to return and write a report. Through this exercise, instructors can spot deficiencies quickly and can take corrective action if needed.

Other lectures focus on drugs in the workplace, drinking, gambling, and the gathering and marking of evidence. Roping and entrapment are the topic of another lecture. It is generally conceded that there is a very fine line where roping ends and entrapment begins. To enhance this distinction and to give the student further insight into the art of roping, the textbook is augmented by a reenacted roping scene that has been professionally directed and edited on videotape.

On the third day, the second part of the undercover training film is shown, and a demonstration of the use of ultraviolet crayons and black light is given.

The fourth day of the course features a lecture on how to build a cover story. Staging is also discussed in the event that students will need this procedure during their undercover career. After the lecture on cover stories, students complete a typical employment application and present themselves to the trainer as a job applicant. The trainer, playing the role of personnel manager, picks apart the applicant's story and the application form. This exercise gives students firsthand experience of what they might encounter in the real world.

The first half of the fifth day is devoted to winding up the training school with a critique of the course, a group discussion of *The Big Decision*, and any remaining general investigation cases that must be discussed with trainers. The students are then given a final examination to determine how much of the material they have been able to absorb during the week. The results of this final examination are made available to the students' employers for future guidance. The students are free to contact the instructors in the future should they need advice with a particular problem.

Benefits of Training

Experience has shown that formalized training pays off in terms of increased safety for the agent, greater likelihood of winning criminal prosecutions and labor arbitrations, and improved professionalism in the security department. Students who do well in the training program usually turn out to be productive agents, whereas those who do poorly are generally not successful after returning to their companies.

Most college graduates who embark on this training are willing to do undercover work, especially if they believe that it will lead to a higher position in the near future. Some students become so enthralled with their ability at undercover work that they are content to remain in the position indefinitely. Outstanding agents who really enjoy their work are worth more to their employer than even their immediate supervisor. Unfortunately, it is impossible to identify these unique people in advance; only the true test of field undercover work can make that determination.

FINANCIAL MATTERS

One of the less dramatic aspects of the undercover agent's training, but one that can become quite important to the success of an operation, is the handling of expense reports, payroll checks, and funds earned incidental to the investigation. These topics are discussed in this section.

Expense Reports

In an undercover case, the operative must be allowed a nominal amount each month to cover entertainment, bar expenses, gambling debts, and so on. If the operative simply records these expenses on an expense report, they might be misinterpreted by the accounting clerk who processes the document. If the expense report falls into the wrong hands, the integrity of the undercover assignment could be destroyed. Therefore, the operative should use a prearranged code to record telltale items like bar expenses and gambling debts on the expense report.

To ensure that undercover trainees retain their instructions about expenses, it is recommended that they complete a sample expense report for a full week. The report should include every conceivable entry that might come up in the following years. Trainees should also be instructed on how to record the payment of union dues and initiation fees if they must join a union as part of an investigation.

Payroll Checks

Operatives employed by private agencies are often required to report to the central agency office to pick up their payroll check. Depending on the circumstances of the assignment, this might be an acceptable practice. Of course, police officers working undercover should never be required to pick up their pay at the police station.

It is often possible to have the undercover agent's payroll or expense checks mailed directly to his or her home. If a possible mail watch is of concern, such as with law enforcement agents, the payroll department can send the check directly to the agent's bank for deposit. This will not require the agent's handling, and the funds will always be available.

Payroll and Benefit Records

Computerized payroll and group benefit records are another complication for undercover work. Many corporations input all payroll and employee benefit information into a central computer, which outlying plants or divisions can access. In this case, the only way to avoid compromising the investigation is to delete the agent from the centralized computer records. If the agent's identity is later fed into the main computer by a local employer, it must again be deleted before the agent can move on to another assignment.

A question that sometimes arises is that of responsibility for workers' compensation claims. If an operative from an outside agency is injured on the job, who assumes the burden of the claim—the company or the outside agency? The operative's claim should be processed as it would be for any other company worker. The case could be compromised if the claim is sent back to the agency's insurance company.

Funds from Outside Sources

When operatives work for a security agency, it is common practice for them to keep whatever pay they receive at the client's place of business. The agency supplements this pay to bring it up to a stated minimum and gives the agent an additional sum for each daily report.

Many companies that retain undercover agents on their corporate staff follow this system, but others prefer to pay the agent a stated salary from corporate headquarters. Any pay that the agent receives locally is returned directly to the corporate security department and used to defray the overall cost of the investigation. Naturally, if the local money received is in the form of a payroll check, the operative must cash the check, preferably where other employees cash their checks. The check should never be endorsed over to the corporation itself.

Because of the tax problems that arise with an operation of this type, someone in the payroll department must be privy to the undercover program. This person must scan the local payroll check stub for tax withholdings before determining the withholding from the corporate payroll check. If this is not done, the company invariably ends up paying more than necessary to the federal government for tax and Social Security, creating problems for the agent at tax time.

This procedure is useful when a company undercover investigator goes to work on another company's payroll for a short time to build a cover story. It is, of course, also useful for law enforcement agents who have to take outside employment to maintain their cover story.

New Identity

The Social Security Administration allows investigators to change their name but still retain the same Social Security number so as not to lose any credits to their account. The form for declaring a pseudonym (assumed name) is available from any Social Security Administration office. A note of caution for agents working on foreign (secondary) payrolls for the cover: These agents must pick up a copy of their withholding statement upon termination of the cover employment to avoid entanglement when filing income tax. Normally, the sum of the withholding statements from all other employers and the adjusted withholding statement from the agent's corporate headquarters should, if proper procedures have been set up, equal the agent's annual salary.

At least one state, Illinois, has established a procedure whereby an agent can assume a new identity. Once the agent has obtained a new Social Security card, the company can apply to the Secretary of State's office for a new driver's license for the agent. This procedure should only be used as a last resort; it is fraught with potential complications regarding employee benefits, Social Security credits to the bogus number, and so on.

GAMBLING

An informal survey of security practitioners regarding gambling problems reveals that in-plant gambling has declined somewhat since the early eighties. This is due, in part, to the growth in many areas of legalized gambling, including state-run lottery programs and gambling casinos on Indian reservations, river boats, and sea-going ships. The state of New York has a well-established Off Track Betting (OTB) system that enables gamblers to bet on horse races from betting parlors throughout the state. Gamblers have come to trust these state-run programs to provide correct payoffs, so the only advantage left to organized crime is the promptness of a winning payoff.

Despite its decline in popularity, in-plant gambling still occurs in some places. Various versions of the numbers racket continue to plague U.S. companies. In a numbers operation, the winning three-digit number is usually taken from pari-mutuel figures obtained from the racetracks or from the financial pages of the local newspaper. In some instances, however, the winning number is selected through a drawing, as in the policy operations common to Chicago or the bolita operations in Hispanic areas of the United States.

Investigators should be thoroughly familiar with the local gambling custom and with the method by which the collections are gathered. They should know how bets are recorded, how payoffs are made, and related information. For new agents who have not had the benefit of formal training in either a police academy or an academic setting, a training program must cover the topic of illegal gambling. Once investigators are familiar with the general mechanics of the gambling operation, they can learn how to seize physical evidence that will later prove a gambling pattern.

In the numbers racket, which is quite common in many industrial plants in eastern cities, one or more people might control the gambling operation in a particular plant. The larger the plant, the greater the likelihood of more than one numbers operation. Some numbers rackets in industrial plants have a daily "take" of $50 to several hundred dollars. If you consider that many number "plays" are nickel, dime, or quarter plays, you can appreciate the volume generated on any one day.

In operations like this, it is not uncommon to find that the principal operator has enlisted the help of one or more fellow employees to act as "runners" so that all bets and money can be taken. This, of course, necessitates that the operator or the runners make daily rounds of the various departments of the plant. In a large numbers operation, the operator frequently transfers the recorded bets picked up by the runners to one master sheet, which he carries with him until he has the opportunity to phone in the bets for permanent recording. The undercover investigator can often find the runners' discarded slips of paper in rest room trash cans, in factory refuse containers, and so on.

Many of the bets are handled entirely by interdepartmental telephone. The agent should be alert to employees who spend a great deal of their time receiving telephone calls during the morning. In most eastern cities, numbers bets must generally be recorded by 1:00 P.M. Therefore, the bets are usually phoned in during the noon hour. With horse race bets, the deadline for betting is set by the particular racetrack.

Investigators should also be alert to evidence of other forms of gambling within the plant, including U.S. Treasury Balance pools, athletic event pools, syndicated gambling cards for baseball and football games, crap games, and card games. These forms of gambling are less common than numbers or horse betting, which are operated on a daily basis.

Once the undercover agent identifies those who are involved in the gambling operation, it is usually an easy matter to secure physical evidence (Figures 3.1 to 3.5). The agent should place the slips of paper in envelopes and should note on each envelope the time, date, and place of discovery; the contents of the envelope; and the agent's identification number.

CASE 1: SKOKIE, ILLINOIS

After a number of months of undercover activity, the agent became aware of one employee who seemed to have a corner on all of the policy bets within the plant. (Policy bets are a form of the numbers racket.) The agent noticed that the employee was away from his workstation regularly for several hours and was seen visiting employees in other sections of the building. At break time, coins and slips of paper were frequently passed to this employee in the lunch room and in the men's rest room.

THESE ARE CLASSIC SYMPTOMS OF A NUMBERS OPERA-TION. THE AGENT SHOULD ALWAYS BE ALERT TO THEM.

After making these observations, the agent set out to become friendly with the suspect. He placed regular policy bets with him.

As the two men were leaving the plant together in the suspect's car, the agent was pleasantly surprised to discover that the suspect drove several blocks to a public telephone that he could operate from the seat of his automobile. The subject called in a long series of policy bets that he had recorded on a slip of paper. After telephoning, he crumpled the paper and threw it out the window, and the two men drove back to the plant.

Figure 3.1. Numbers slips recovered by an undercover agent in Bridgeport, Connecticut (see Case 2). The slip at top center shows plays on "lead numbers."

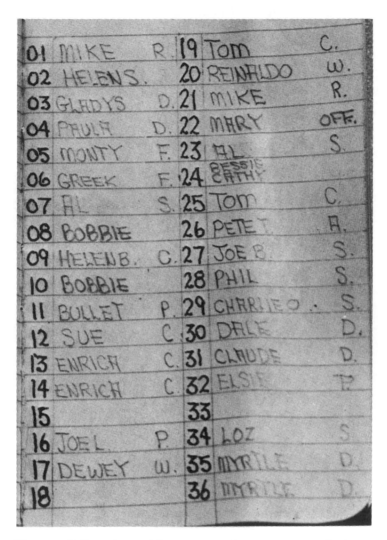

Figure 3.2. A gambling operator's master record of employee-players in a daily pool based on U.S. Treasury reports. Employees were assigned one or more two-digit numbers and were identified by first name and department letter. The booklet was seized during an inspection of lockers prior to the "bust." The undercover agent revealed its location.

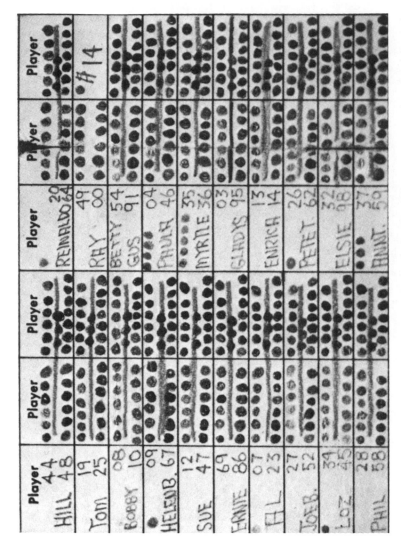

Figure 3.3. The addition record of the U.S. Treasury Department pool. Note that each player has two numbers. Dots in the second and third columns represent individual "plays" for each number, and dots in the "Name" column represent "hits."

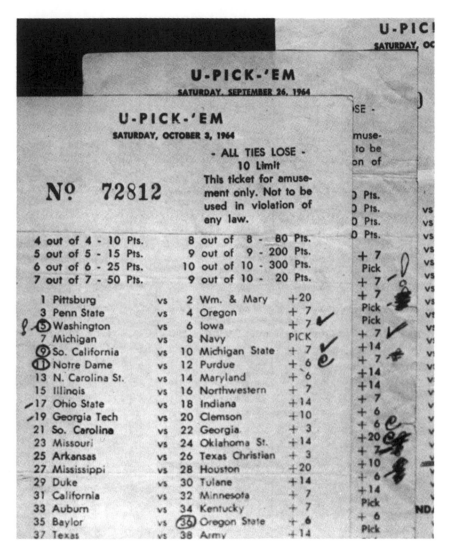

Figure 3.4. Syndicated football cards recovered by an undercover agent. Each selection cost a quarter, with a minimum of four games. The lowest possible payoff was $10. The printed admonishment against gambling is merely a thinly veiled cover against possible arrest.

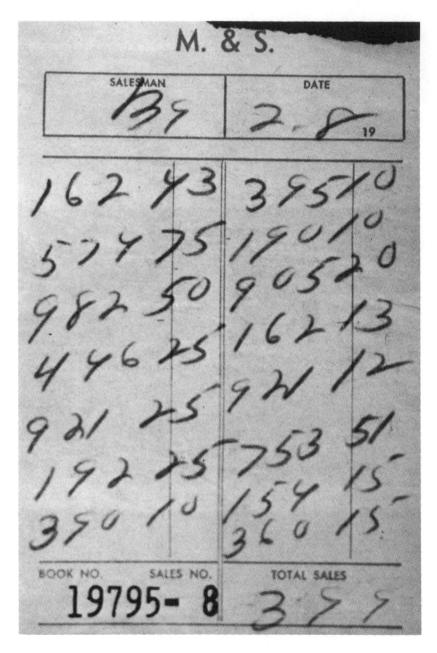

Figure 3.5. Numbers action in Northumberland County, Pennsylvania, disguised as a sales slip. Plays ranged from a dime to 75¢. This evidence was seized in an unannounced locker inspection.

The retrieval of these papers from the public telephone area by other security agents was quickly established as routine. Eventually, the operator of the policy racket became so nonchalant about his actions that he passed the paper with the recorded policy bets to the undercover agent and instructed him to throw it out the window. It was a simple matter for the agent to fake the throw and palm the crumpled slip, which was later preserved as evidence.

The suspect was eventually apprehended while telephoning in the policy bets. The exact location of the policy wheel was turned over to the Chicago Police Department, which was able to raid that location.

In-plant gambling operators seldom bankroll the operation themselves. Occasionally, small-time numbers operators accept bets on the "lead numbers" (the first and/or second number of the three-digit series) and bankroll these bets because they are generally low bets that carry low payoff rates, such as 4 to 1 or 8 to 1. Operators of a syndicated numbers racket occasionally operate their own independent numbers operation with a lower payoff rate; in these cases, the bank is maintained on company premises. On several occasions, security officers have raided and seized numbers banks on company premises that totaled several hundred dollars.

However, this is more of a pool operation, with a small cut going to the operator. In theory, athletic pools arranged within employee groups are free of any profit taking by the operator, but in reality, it is quite common to find that the athletic pools are often rigged to give the operator a better chance than the other players in the pool.

CASE 2: BRIDGEPORT, CONNECTICUT

The undercover agent's suspicions were aroused by the shipping clerk in a large manufacturing plant. The clerk was obviously taking telephone bets on the numbers from other employees during the morning hours. On several occasions, the undercover operative was able to answer the telephone and, in this way, get a good "feel" as to the extent of the action. The shipping clerk regularly took his action from the plant to a nearby tavern, where he used a public telephone to call in the bets. The undercover agent could not get close enough to the telephone booth to determine the number to which the call was being made.

However, it soon became apparent that the shipping clerk was also taking horse race bets, which he called in from his shipping office in the plant during the early afternoon. By visiting the office at the appropriate time on a number of occasions over several weeks, the undercover agent was able to piece together the exact number that the clerk dialed. A quick check of the telephone number revealed it to be the shipping clerk's home number. The house was being used as a central banking point for a gambling syndicate in the county. This information was passed on to the intelligence division of the Internal Revenue Service for follow-up and appropriate action.

The shipping clerk was apprehended one day at noon as he was on his way to the tavern. On his person was approximately $187 in bills and coins and a piece of paper showing the total numbers action for that day (see Figure 3.1).

DRUGS

In recent years, the use of narcotics and dangerous drugs has affected virtually every company in the United States to some degree. Experience has shown that the use of drugs, including marijuana, has an adverse effect on both the worker and the company. Workers' compensation cases costing tens of thousands of dollars sometimes arise in plants that have problems with illegal drug use. Absenteeism, tardiness, and employee mistakes are another result of drug use. Generally, whenever large-scale gambling or illicit traffic in drugs is prevalent in an industrial plant, it is accompanied by the theft of company property.

Many firms have instituted preemployment drug screening. However, without a policy of random on-the-job retesting, such preemployment programs have little impact. The body purges itself within 30 days of any drug residues that are normally picked up by a urinalysis. A few companies use a saliva exam (the "spit test") to detect the smoking of marijuana during breaks and lunch periods. This test, developed by UCLA scientists, is valid for a four-hour period after smoking. However, its use has not caught on in U.S. industry. Obviously, a complete approach to the problem of on-the-job drug use must include the use of undercover agents.

Many drugs are dispensed on company property in glassine envelopes or plastic bags. Marijuana cigarettes, or "joints," are frequently contained in regular cigarette packages, such as flip-top boxes. Marijuana cigarettes are occasionally disguised with legitimate cigarette papers and filters. The tobacco is removed from a filter-tip cigarette and replaced with marijuana. The only obvious difference is that the end of the cigarette paper is twisted to prevent the marijuana from escaping. When placed filter tip up in a normal cigarette package, the marijuana cigarettes are difficult to distinguish from regular cigarettes.

The most common drugs found in industrial plants and private companies today are marijuana, hashish (hash), and methamphetamine (speed). As a rule, the harder drugs—heroin, morphine, and cocaine—are usually not present in great quantity. These drugs adversely affect the worker's performance to the extent that their use would be obvious to even the most inexperienced observer. Workers who use drugs generally lean toward stimulants from the amphetamine family or hallucinogens like marijuana or hashish. The use of LSD in the workplace is rare.

The Drug Enforcement Administration (DEA) provides the following glossary of slang terms for drugs. Many of these terms are commonly heard in the private employment sector.

Amphetamines: Beans, bennies, black beauties, black mollies, copilots, crank, crossroads, crystal dexies, double cross, meth, minibennies, pep pills, rosas, roses, speed, thru truck drivers, uppers, wake-ups, whites.

Barbiturates: Barbs, blockbusters, bluebirds, blue devils, blues, Christmas trees, downers, green dragons, Mexican reds, nebbies, nimbies, pajaro rojo, pink ladies, pinks, rainbows, reds, red and blues, redbirds, red devils, sleeping pills, stumblers, yellow jackets, yellows.

Cocaine: Blow, C, coca, coke, crack, dust, flake, girl, heaven, lady, mujer, nose candy, paradise, perico, polvo blanco, rock, snow, white.

Hashish: Goma do mota, hash, soles.

Heroin: Big H, boy, brown, brown sugar, caballo, chiva, crap, estuffa, H, heronia, hombre, horse, junk, Mexican mud, polvo, scag, smack, stuff, thing.

LSD: Acid, blotter acid, California sunshine, haze, microdots, paper acid, purple haze, sunshine, wedges, window panes.

Marijuana: Acapulco gold, cannabis, Colombian, ganga, grass, griffa, hemp, herb, J, jay, joint, Mary Jane, mota, mutah, Panama red, pot, reefer, sativa, smoke, stick, tea, weed, yerba.

Peyote: Buttons, cactus, mesc, mescal, mescal buttons.

Methaqualone: Quaalude, quads, quas, soapers, so pes, sopor.

Morphine: Cube, first line, goma, morf, morfina, morpho, morphy, mud.

Phencyclidine: Angel dust, crystal, cyclone, hog, PCP, peace pill, rocket fuel, supergrass, tic tac.

Undercover agents must know the slang terms currently used for various illegal drugs in their locale. In addition, they should recognize illegal drugs when they encounter them and should be able to make "buys," preserving the drugs for future evidence.

If drugs are present in the workplace, the undercover agent's prime objective is to gather evidence of drug traffic and use. This is normally done by making buys. The agent should have no difficulty buying a joint of marijuana or some capsules of speed. Any drugs purchased should be preserved for evidence and later used in an interrogation.

Certain legal considerations must be taken into account when making buys or even possessing illicit drug contraband. In the state of Georgia, for example, it is against the law to purchase illegal drugs. In other states, you can be arrested for possession of an illegal substance. New agents must understand what can go wrong if they are caught up in these circumstances. For example, an auto accident on the way home from work on the day of a "buy" might very well land the agent in jail. The agent's handler can probably intercede with the police to sidetrack any prosecution, but in the process there is a great likelihood that the agent's cover will be blown.

The only practical approach is for the agent's supervisors to arrange a clearance for such activity with the proper police authority. Traditionally, the police have exhibited little interest in use of minor amounts of marijuana in the industrial setting. They are usually content to let the operative proceed without any further police involvement and allow the case to be closed by the company's own security manager.

However, sales within the company of cocaine, other hard drugs, or large amounts of marijuana are a different matter. When the police do not have sufficient human resources to send in their own in-plant operative, they will usually allow the undercover person to act as their own agent. Some police officials will want the agent to immediately turn in to them any "buys" made in the plant. Others will accept the agent's marking and preservation of the drug contraband and even permit the agent to hold the evidence until the end of the case.

If good police relations have been established, the company security manager may be able to conclude the theft portion of the case at the same time the police close up the drug facet. In this way, neither party's case will be affected by premature action on the other's part.

The biggest problem encountered by undercover agents today will be in participating with suspected employees in social gatherings where marijuana or hash are regularly used. A number of agents claim that they can simulate taking a "drag" on a joint as it is passed around in such a group.

The experience of most legitimate undercover operatives shows that an agent is seldom accepted by a pot-smoking group unless the group believes that the agent is a marijuana user; the group will not accept someone who they think is "straight." Once rejected, it may become impossible for the agent to gather physical evidence of marijuana use. This creates a dilemma for the security directory: should the agent be allowed to participate if he or she is not able to successfully simulate the act of marijuana smoking? There is no easy answer for this and each security manager will have to make an individual decision.

Many agents also claim that they can feign euphoria or simulate heightened physical activity as a result of taking a "hit" of speed.

The problem with these activities is that when the agent is cross-examined in court, prior drug use is almost always brought up to impeach or discredit the agent's testimony. Agents who make good witnesses are often able to convince arbitrators or judges that they did not, in fact, take drugs and only simulated their use.

On the other hand, there are many successful agents who have had no prior experience with drugs, including marijuana, yet were able to infiltrate social groups without using or feigning the use of drugs.

Professional security administrators certainly do not want their security agents to become drug users, nor do they want to see the agents' court testimony impeached or discredited. On the other hand, agents are faced with the task of infiltrating employee groups that see nothing wrong with the social use of softer drugs. Without question, this presents a very delicate problem in formulating policy.

MARKING EVIDENCE

In the earlier section on gambling, a method of marking and pre-serving evidence in envelopes was suggested. This procedure can also be used to preserve evidence of illegal drug trafficking. Un-dercover agents sometimes need to mark caches of merchandise hidden on company property, awaiting removal in a theft case. An ideal method of marking such property is with a fluorescent crayon, but adequate markings can also be made with an ordinary ballpoint pen without compromising the investigation.

When an agent marks for future evidence a cache of stolen merchandise or other company property, the agent's daily report should reflect exactly what was marked, the manner in which it was marked, and where the distinguishing marks were placed. By carefully describing how the evidence was marked, it is possible to have a completely tight presentation of physical evidence at a sub-sequent trial, arbitration, or other proceeding. Likewise, with the recovery of any physical evidence of gambling or drugs, the de-tails of the recovery and marking of evidence must be reported completely in the daily report. It is often possible to recover stolen property that the undercover agent has marked, and this later be-comes the basis of a specific criminal complaint for larceny.

Sometimes, an undercover agent, working with another in-vestigator assigned to outside surveillance, is able to recover evi-dence of property that is in the process of being stolen. This is illustrated by the following case.

CASE 3: PITTSBURGH, PENNSYLVANIA

After several weeks of effort, the undercover agent was in-vited to join a group of employees who met regularly at a nearby tavern immediately after work. Each evening, the shop steward entered the bar carrying a small brown paper bag that was rolled shut at the top. Based on his previous observations of the shop steward, the undercover agent surmised that the bag contained stolen merchandise from the plant.

Working with another security investigator who was assigned to outside surveillance, the undercover agent arranged to substitute a bag of fruit that was exactly the same type and size as the bag of stolen merchandise. While the undercover agent diverted the shop steward's attention at the bar, the second agent made the switch by picking up the bag of stolen merchandise and leaving the bag of fruit. Of course, the shop steward discovered the switch that evening, but he concluded that it had been an honest mistake by another patron of the bar. He asked the bartender to be on the lookout for his bag in case it was returned.

Ultimately, the bag of stolen merchandise became the basis for a specific criminal complaint of larceny filed against the shop steward (Figure 3.6).

ONE OF THE GREAT DIFFICULTIES IN ANY INDUSTRIAL THEFT CASE IS PROVING THE *CORPUS DELICTI* (THE SUBSTANTIAL AND FUNDAMENTAL FACT NEEDED TO PROVE THE COMMISSION OF A CRIME). IN THIS CASE, THE *CORPUS DELICTI* COULD BE ESTABLISHED WITHOUT DOUBT, THUS OVERCOMING THE BIGGEST HURDLE IN LARCENY CASES.

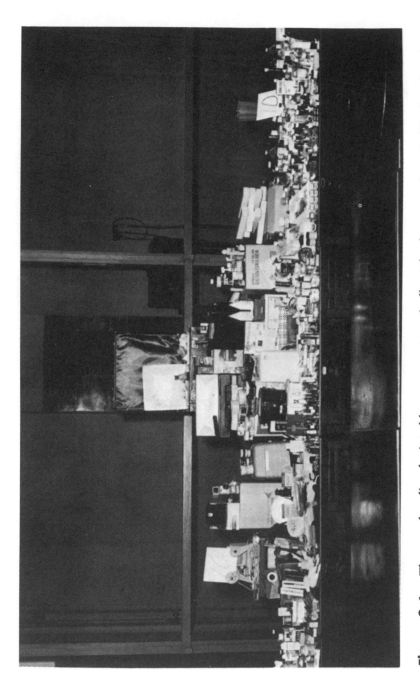

Figure 3.6. The merchandise depicted here was systematically stolen by an employee in Pittsburgh, using a shopping bag stuffed with newspapers on the top.

4

The Cover

The most important factor in a successful undercover operation—
whether it is an industrial investigation or a covert intelligence
operation—is the cover story. Deficiencies in training, the art of
roping, knowledge of the laws of entrapment, and other areas can
all be overcome to some degree. However, if the undercover agent
is to be believed and the operation is to be successful, the cover
must hold up to scrutiny.

The typical industrial or law enforcement undercover case
need not be set up with the "staging" and the usual "deep cover"
that most international espionage cases require. However, sufficient cover must be set up and maintained for the investigation to
succeed. The elaborateness of cover needed will depend on the
circumstances of the case and, of course, on budgetary and time
constraints.

Undercover investigators often work on a foreign (outside)
payroll while establishing their cover. This might be a job in a local
restaurant, tavern, or hamburger stand. A job like this might last
from several weeks to several months. (The pay that the agent receives should be handled as described in Chapter 3.)

In an article on industrial undercover work, Morton M. Hunt (1961) stated:

> To build and maintain a successful "cover" story calls for planning and discipline; it takes some doing for a lad just out of Harvard Business School to act the part of restaurant busboy without spilling the beans. An operator must wear clothes appropriate to his station, perhaps live in a dreary furnished room, and spend evenings with his fellow employees at the bowling alley though he might prefer to be home listening to the "Missa Solemnis."

This advice, although decades old, holds true today.

To facilitate the establishment of a proper cover story, undercover trainees at McKesson Corporation were given blank application forms and told to establish what they felt would be a proper cover. The instructor reviewed each application with the trainee, pointing out the weaknesses and loopholes of the written cover story.

As pointed out in the beginning of this chapter, the cover story is all-important. The agent is living a double life and, to be successful, must adhere to the cover story first laid out. If it is unusual in nature or perhaps unbelievable, the agent may eventually trip himself or herself up. To avoid this, undercover agents have always been taught the "three musts" for any cover story:

1. The story must be simple.
2. The story must be believable.
3. The story must be as true to the operative's real life as possible.

SETTLING IN THE NEW CITY

Before beginning a new assignment, undercover agents must develop a good knowledge of the area in which they will be working. They must be familiar with the local bars, hangouts, rackets, and so on. They must immediately develop a complete local identification, including a local driver's license and local plates for their automobile.

If the undercover agent is native to the city in which the operation will take place, problems related to the cover story are minimized. With a large corporation that has facilities in more than 250 locations from coast to coast, it is a different matter. Security work for a big company requires a certain mobility on the part of the undercover agents.

At McKesson, operatives were advised to obtain local employment with another company as soon as they arrived in the new city. They were generally encouraged to hold this employment for at least 30 days. This gave them an opportunity to explore the city. The operatives took advantage of the public transportation system, if any, spending their off-hours riding various bus or subway routes. They were also encouraged to use an automobile to learn the major streets and sections of the city. Their goal was to be able to move about with some degree of familiarity later in the investigation.

Operatives were also advised to scan back issues of the local newspapers for the period that they were supposed to have lived in the city. Seldom, if ever, were agents instructed to pass themselves off as natives of the city; instead, they were to make it appear that they had been in town for some time. Consequently, a job of 30 days in a restaurant was easily altered to make it appear that the investigator had been in the city for three or four months.

Many private agencies do not give their operatives sufficient time to develop a good cover in a new city. It is not uncommon to hear of covers being established over a weekend before the agent applies for a job.

GETTING HIRED

Unlike the informal infiltration of a criminal gang, industrial undercover work involves a certain initial formality that the agent must pass without jeopardizing the cover: getting hired. It is impossible to list every conceivable obstacle related to getting hired, but here are a few: layoffs with provisions for seniority recall, departmental seniority, job bidding, union hiring halls, the preferences of the personnel interviewer, and IQ and aptitude tests. All of these serve to test the ingenuity and imagination of the security director.

The existence of an undercover investigation should be controlled on a "need-to-know" basis. No exceptions to this rule should be permitted. What role, then, should the plant manager play in the hiring process? Can agents gain employment on their own, or should the plant manager be asked to assist? Should the personnel manager be brought into the investigation to facilitate the agent's hiring? Should another executive be taken into confidence to place the agent in the proper department and on the correct shift? Such questions constantly arise. They are complicated by the effect on executive morale when some members of the executive group are briefed about the undercover project, and others are not.

Experience has shown that investigations are usually most successful when knowledge of the operation is limited to one top executive. Even this person should not be told the agent's name except on a need-to-know basis. Investigations directors are in a better position to control the investigation if only they know the agent's identity. If the agent can gain employment without assistance, so much the better. If not, then the top executive might have to contact the personnel manager directly, even if it means passing over one or more other line managers in the chain of command.

In terms of getting assigned to a particular department or shift, it is best to have agents attempt this on their own, even if it means an additional delay of weeks or months. In the meantime, agents should use their employment by the target organization to strengthen their cover. Much valuable information can be gained from fellow employees during lunch and break periods. After hours, the agent's work may just be beginning in the neighborhood tavern across from the plant gates! The transfer of agents from department to department can be detrimental, especially if this is unusual for new employees.

Union hiring halls present a major obstacle, but they can be circumvented if time permits. Undercover agents gain a tremendous advantage when they arrive on the job with impeccable credentials and a cover that is virtually foolproof—one given by the dispatcher at the union hiring hall. It is not uncommon for union day laborers to attempt to win favor with dispatchers and receive choice assignments of a more permanent nature. The investigations director need only understand the psychology of such people to take advantage and allow the agent to gain placement.

APPLYING FOR THE POSITION

The undercover operative must take several factors into consideration when filling out the application form. Generally, some adjustment must be made for age so that the operative appears to be about the same age as most new hires. Another factor that must be considered is education. If company requirements call for a minimum of a high school education, operatives are encouraged to eliminate any reference to college. To account for the agent's time in college, the length of the agent's prior employment or military service can be expanded.

The matter of references should be decided on an individual basis, based on the employment practices at the particular location. The type of past employment shown on the application should generally be similar in nature to the job for which the agent is applying. When a McKesson agent was applying for a position in a drug warehouse, previous employment with another company unit or a competitor was never shown. If experience in the drug field seemed desirable and the operative had had such experience, then it was an easy matter to show this experience under the heading of military service.

Years ago, many companies had a section on their application headed "Wages Expected" or something similar. When applying for a job in a union plant, undercover operatives were instructed to write in this space, "Union scale." To a union member in the personnel office, this response carried a message of its own. Although no longer relevant today, this example is presented to show new agents how the application process can be used as a first step in roping and to strengthen the cover story.

If the application process involves screening tests, the undercover agent's target test scores must be decided in advance. The agent should be given sufficient copies of the test on which to practice. If the company uses a paper-and-pencil honesty test during preemployment screening, special arrangements must be made to ensure that the agent is not rejected because of a low score. Many undercover agents have difficulty obtaining a qualifying score on these tests.

The following might seem to be an insignificant point, but it is made for the benefit of new or inexperienced undercover operatives. Some new operatives, attempting to follow through with the rule of "dressing the part," forget that when applying for a job they should try to make the best possible impression. In other words, what might later be acceptable and proper dress for mixing with other workers might make a poor impression on the local personnel manager. In one case, an operative dressed for the interview as he had observed the employees dressed on their noon break. However, the personnel manager did not hire him because of his appearance. It mattered little that he was dressed just like the current employees at the plant. The personnel manager expected a better appearance for the interview.

HANDLING CREDIT

The establishment of local credit might seem like a relatively minor point but, if not handled correctly, can be the undoing of the undercover operative. Despite proper coaching, new agents sometimes reveal their identity to someone, such as an automobile salesperson, when they are trying to obtain credit. Regardless of promises to the contrary, the credit department or the finance company will invariably call the target company, seeking to verify the employment of Jay Doe, Company Investigator. It only takes one telephone call of this type to terminate the agent's assignment.

For this reason, new operatives must understand that attempts to establish credit must be based solely on their salary as an ordinary worker and on their actual time on the local job. Obtaining credit might be difficult, but there is little alternative unless major credit purchases are made in another city where the agent's true identity would not hamper the investigation.

New agents must understand that they are leading two lives:

1. The life of an agent, as recognized by superiors
2. The life of a warehouse worker, truck driver, or whatever the undercover assignment requires

For credit purposes, these two lives must never cross. There must never be any connecting trail from one life to the other. Therefore, agents who intend to use their true identity and job status for credit purposes in their home community must never reveal their city of origin during an undercover operation. An agent whose home is Montgomery, Alabama, should never refer to that city while working undercover assignments in other parts of the country, especially if the agent has applied for credit in Montgomery under his or her true identity.

To better understand the hazards involved in credit applications, undercover agents need to have some idea of how the credit-reporting system works. At present, there are three major credit-reporting agencies in the United States: T.R.W. Credit Data, Trans-Union, and Equifax. In addition, there are many local and regional bureaus. The three national credit-reporting agencies and the local and regional bureaus cooperate with one another in exchanging information. It is possible to identify a credit applicant with only a name and a city. The addition of a former address or a Social Security number narrows the search that much more.

Suppose that a retailer in St. Louis, Missouri, inquires about the credit background of our hypothetical agent from Montgomery, Alabama. If the agent once purchased an automobile on credit in Montgomery and the St. Louis retailer discovers the agent's Montgomery background, the cover is blown. This is why agents must separate their two lives for credit purposes.

For the undercover director, there is one saving grace in all this. There is no nationwide computer bank that identifies people by name and Social Security number. It is imperative for someone making inquiries to be able to narrow down the search to one or two geographic areas.

SPECIAL NEEDS OF FEMALE OPERATIVES

Female undercover operatives who attempt to operate nationwide encounter unique problems. It is not uncommon for men to drift from city to city, easily making acquaintances and friends in restaurants and bars. For women, the situation is slightly more difficult. Accordingly, it is customary for female operatives to be given additional time to establish their cover story. This is well illustrated in the following case.

CASE 4: CINCINNATI, OHIO

Upon arriving in the city, the undercover operative located an apartment through a real estate agency within commuting distance of the downtown area. After securing the apartment, a telephone, and a driver's license, she found employment as a cocktail waitress in a downtown bar that, according to reputation, was frequented by many members of the local underworld.

While working in the bar for several months, the operative become aware of every racket that prevailed in the city, and she could identify most of the leading members of the local crime establishment. Realizing that her job as a cocktail waitress in this bar might prevent her from obtaining employment at the desired business, the operative upgraded her cover by working briefly as a salesclerk in a downtown store.

From this second job, the operative was able to make the transition to her desired objective. Once established in her main assignment, she could use the many contacts she had established as a cocktail waitress to further her acceptance by the less desirable employees she encountered. Many of the people involved in thefts from the company were acquainted with the same criminals that the operative had come to know at the bar. Therefore, she was readily accepted into the inner circle of thievery.

IT'S A SMALL WORLD

Many people feel that the size of large cities enhances their anonymity. Generally, this is true, but as the following case illustrates, it really is "a small world."

CASE 5: MEMPHIS, TENNESSEE

A relatively inexperienced investigator was assigned to a case in Memphis. He had been in the city several weeks and had succeeded in accomplishing the normal preliminary steps in establishing a cover. He had set up a post office box to which his first paycheck was directed. Upon receiving the paycheck, he went to one of the large banks in the city and tried to cash the check by using his corporate security identification card.

> NORMALLY, INVESTIGATORS SHOULD NEVER CARRY AN IDENTIFICATION CARD WHEN ACTING IN AN UNDERCOVER ROLE. THIS INVESTIGATOR HAS JUST CROSSED HIS TWO LIVES!

As it happened, the teller was the girlfriend of a junior executive who was employed at the location of the agent's upcoming assignment. The agent made the additional mistake of attempting to make a date with the teller, ensuring that she would not forget him.

It's easy to imagine the reception the agent received three weeks later when he applied for a job in connection with his assignment. To avoid these problems, the agent should have first opened a checking account at the bank with a cash deposit and then later used bank-by-mail envelopes to deposit his payroll and expense checks. Then his company checks would have been mixed with the thousands of others that the bank's bookkeeping department routinely processes. These checks never receive individual scrutiny, and no one in the accounting department is given the opportunity to match up a face with a check.

MOVING HOUSEHOLD GOODS

Everything that undercover operatives do should be carefully thought out in advance. Will the action jeopardize the operative's cover? The movement of household goods and the necessary communication with nationwide moving companies is a common hazard.

Most moving companies are only too happy to deal directly with large companies to move their employees' household goods. To reduce the possibility that the moving company will expose the cover story, the undercover operative should follow these simple procedures:

1. When dealing with the moving company at the point of origin, always represent yourself as being self-employed.
2. The moving company will not unload your furniture at the destination unless paid for in advance or guaranteed by a company purchase order. Therefore, you must be advanced sufficient cash to cover the moving company's fees.
3. At the destination, again represent yourself as being self-employed.

The following case illustrates the problem that might arise when these procedures are not followed.

CASE 6: PEORIA, ILLINOIS

In Minneapolis, the point of origin, the investigator told the moving company that he was self-employed. He preceded his family to the destination. In the interim, his wife received a telephone call from a local representative of the nationwide moving company, who asked, "Where can our driver contact your husband upon arrival of the furniture in Peoria?" The agent's wife gave the representative the name of the company where her husband was to be employed undercover.

When the furniture arrived in Peoria, this information was picked up by the local representative, who promptly telephoned the company. Fortunately, the call was received by the manager of the local plant, and he was privy to the undercover operation. The call came when the switchboard was closed down for lunch, his secretary was gone, and one of the trunk lines was connected directly to his extension. Had anyone else received the call, the agent's cover would have been blown. Another agent would have had to be assigned to the case, increasing the cost of the investigation tremendously.

THE MORAL HERE IS SIMPLE: THINK, THINK, THINK. IS ANY CONTEMPLATED ACTION APT TO BLOW THE AGENT'S COVER?

STAGING

In his book, *The Spymasters of Israel*, Stewart Steven (1980) described the staging of Eli Cohen, Israel's greatest spy. To prepare Cohen for eventual infiltration into Syria, his controllers worked out a cover story that closely matched Cohen's own background. The cover included the fact that he had been born in Beirut, Lebanon, to Syrian parents. The family had purportedly emigrated to Alexandria, Egypt, and had then gone on to Buenos Aires, Argentina. Steven reports that at the time of the staging, there were more than half a million Arabs living in Buenos Aires, many of whom were Syrian. Cohen successfully completed his staging within nine months of his arrival in Argentina. His next step was the penetration itself—Damascus.

When operating a nationwide undercover program, security executives occasionally run into assignments that tax their ingenuity. Such a case occurred in an undercover job in Jackson, Mississippi. There were no southern investigators on the staff who were available for this assignment, and it fell to an investigator from one of the western states. Because Jackson is not the type of city to which people drift from other parts of the United States, extra attention was given to the agent's staging. The following case describes the steps taken to establish a cover and staging for this assignment.

CASE 7: JACKSON, MISSISSIPPI

The undercover agent was first sent to New Orleans, where he spent enough time to become acquainted with the city. From New Orleans, he moved to Jackson. His cover story was that he had gone to New Orleans to see if he could get an athletic scholarship at a local university. After he was turned down, someone suggested that he apply for the same type of scholarship at the local university in Jackson, which also turned him down because of poor grades.

The agent established the usual local cover by obtaining a Mississippi driver's license and Mississippi license plates. He spent many days at the public library reading back copies of the Jackson newspaper to become familiar with the local events of the last six months. He found a job in a drive-in restaurant, where he worked for a number of months. The agent used this job as an employment reference for obtaining work at his assigned location. Even though he obviously spoke with a western accent rather than a southern drawl, his story of attempted schooling in New Orleans and in Jackson was accepted, and ultimately, so was the investigator.

Participating in a mundane, low-level job as part of the staging is quite common even for government agents. Former CIA agent Mike Ackerman (1976) tells the following tale:

In the afternoon I was briefed on my cover story. I was to tell people that I had taken a civilian administrative job at the Department of Defense. I used the story for the first time on Saturday night's date, a girl I had known since graduate school. She was not impressed. "After Dartmouth and Columbia and with your languages, I thought you would have set your sights higher than that." I attempted to appease her by saying that I had only taken the job on an interim basis and was, in fact, awaiting induction into the Air Force. I was going to be an Air Police officer. She looked at me as if I had gone bananas. The truth was that since I hadn't fulfilled my military obligation, the Agency had arranged for me to participate in a special program it had set up with the Air Force. Under the terms of the program I would, upon enlistment, be sent to Officer Training School. Ninety days later, I would be assigned to an air base for about one year. After that, I would be transferred to the Washington area and detailed back to the Agency for the remainder of my obligation. On May 10th I was sworn into the Air Force and put on a plane for Lackland Air Force Base, San Antonio, Texas. For ninety days I marched, made my bed, marched, got my hair cut every three days, marched, memorized chains of command, marched, ran obstacle courses, and marched. I frankly never understood the need for all that marching. For years I had labored under the impression that the Air Force flew.... I've always suspected that I was one of the very few Air Police officers with a Phi Beta Kappa key tucked away under his handcuffs. The Air Force had honored me by selection to its elite unit, the Strategic Air Command. I was assigned to a base in northern California, where my functions were both base police and security. That meant that I got to book drunks and also to baby-sit the H-bomb-laden B-52's and Titan Missiles.... About eight months into my tour of duty we were inspected by a team from SAC Headquarters. One of the visiting colonels reviewed my personnel record and reached a startling conclusion. I was summoned to his office. "Lieutenant, you have a Master's degree. You speak Russian and Spanish and Portuguese. What the hell are you doing in the Air Police? You belong in Intelligence, and I'm going to get right on the phone to Washington and tell them just that." I thanked him profusely but asked him not to interfere, explaining that I was quite happy in the Air Police, which after all, provided me with more of an opportunity than Intelligence would to command troops. I really didn't want him mucking around with my assignment. I was expecting orders back to Washington and the CIA at any time. I got a lecture on how I owed it to the Air Force and the country to exercise my full potential as an officer and how I ought to put personal preferences last. He was still muttering something about complacency when he dismissed me. I don't think he ever made his phone call. In April of 1964, I was reassigned to Washington. For the remainder of my three-year military obligation, I would only put on my uniform for cover reasons—or to take advantage of military discounts on air fares.

The Assignment

5

INFILTRATING THE UNDERWORLD

Many police undercover investigations that attempt to penetrate the underworld meet with failure simply because sufficient time is not set aside for a logical approach to the world of crime. Confirmed criminals, for the most part, do not become professionals overnight. In virtually all cases, professional criminals begin their life of crime at a relatively early age. Through criminal associates and friends, their activities gradually broaden until the individual can be classified as a professional criminal.

The police approach to the infiltration of a criminal gang must be built along similar lines. The infiltration of the gang is begun by operating on and penetrating the fringes of the underworld. Further infiltration can only be done through referrals or references. The better the agent's credentials, the more progress the agent will make in infiltration attempts. By the same token, the more sophisticated the criminal operation, the more unassailable the agent's references must be.

When dealing with the highest levels of an organized crime operation, law enforcement agencies must often be content to rely on informants. A notable exception to this is the FBI's recent success in "turning" members of crime families. In one case, an FBI undercover agent surfaced to testify against the members of his "family." The agent, who had been undercover since he was a young man, had been made a "soldier" of the family.

The infiltration of the ruling council of a national crime organization would require years of effort. Undercover agents of the proper ethnic background must be carefully selected and assigned to the task at an early age. These agents would undoubtedly be required to engage in serious criminal behavior for many years before reaching the upper echelons of the crime organization.

Infiltration of a criminal gang is not unlike the problems encountered by successful businesspeople or politicians: The more contacts you have, the broader your base of support; the better the quality of your contacts, the higher you can go.

The art of roping, which is discussed in Chapter 6, is important to the successful conclusion of a specific case. It also plays an important part in the development of contacts on the fringe of the underworld and in the infiltration of the higher levels of the world of crime.

Infiltration of the underworld is infinitely more difficult than infiltration of an employee group. The techniques are basically similar, but more effort, time, and planning must be devoted to police undercover infiltrations than to the typical private cases encountered in the field of business and industry.

INFILTRATING THE CRIMINAL GANG

Criminal gangs are often very different in nature from each other. This can be influenced by geographic location, ethnic background, local customs, and other factors. Agents must know and understand the type of gang they are to infiltrate—otherwise they will be prone to make little mistakes that eventually add up to nonacceptance by the gang.

Preparation

An undercover agent's training must include ample instruction on the various aspects of the assignment and on techniques for infiltrating the suspect group. Undercover agents are expected to participate in the drinking activities in which other employees engage. Trainees must be educated about the type of drinking that they are apt to encounter and how much they should participate. For example, in at least one eastern city, drinking habits consist of "a shot and a beer" in tandem. In such a situation, the undercover operative should not order a highball. It is permissible and even desirable for operatives to feign slight intoxication, but they must be careful never to overindulge while in the company of suspects.

Agents must also be prepared for the loneliness, boredom, and occasional frustration of undercover work. Unlike their counterparts who work overt investigations, undercover agents must live almost entirely within their cover story. This is particularly hard on professionally oriented criminal justice graduates. They are unable to receive the small but vitally important day-to-day recognition of friends, neighbors, relatives, and fellow workers. This tends to have a discouraging effect not only on the operative, but also on the spouse. Undercover operatives can no longer cultivate friendships with people of their own intellectual level; instead, they must associate daily with ordinary working people and their families. For young, college-trained investigators, this presents morale problems that their supervisor must be aware of and must be prepared to meet.

During preparation for an undercover assignment, operatives must come to accept realistic results of their work. Most industrial plants and warehouses have some security controls, and therefore a minimum of "action" actually occurs on the job. There might be far more action in collateral activities on the street than in the workplace itself. New trainees must understand that they will probably not encounter a theft ring in the plant. The most they can hope for is to observe or learn of individual acts of theft. In general, undercover agents can penetrate established theft rings no more than one case in 10. This is not the fault of the agent or the agent's training.

Common sense dictates that new employees in their twenties will not be invited to join a theft ring comprising workers in their thirties and forties who have worked for the company for 10 or more years. The only time such a situation might develop is if the new worker has a position in the plant that becomes essential to the operation of the ring. It is the individual petty pilferages, however, of which the undercover operative can become aware. These small acts provide the interrogation leverage needed to obtain admissions of guilt. They often lead to admissions of theft ring activity if, in fact, a ring exists.

In other words, new trainees must understand that if their efforts produce even one or two interrogation advantages on any one individual suspect, they have handled the job satisfactorily. The agent should view any additional information developed as a bonus. If, during the course of a six-month investigation, only one incident of employee theft is observed, the assignment has still been successful. Think of what the employee might have stolen during that period when not under surveillance.

These points on expectation of results and premature evaluation of apparently petty suspects are important not only to the agent, but also to the company executive who receives progress reports. Investigation supervisors must take the time to inculcate the proper outlook on the part of the company executives for whom they work. Failure to do so will only bring on misunderstandings, will inevitably shorten the authorized time for the investigation, and might even result in major thieves being incorrectly evaluated and thus permitted to remain on the payroll The only reliable method for evaluating an employee's degree of dishonesty is interrogation based on information developed by the undercover agent, followed by a signed statement that is then verified by polygraph examination.[1] Experience has shown that to make value judgments of any other kind is being naive and foolhardy.

The investigations supervisor should never overlook the agent's motivation (or lack of motivation). It is almost always impossible to motivate a college-trained agent for a permanent life of undercover assignments. The best strategy is continually to emphasize undercover's essential role in security or law enforcement and to suggest that good undercover efforts will be rewarded later with more desirable assignments. Among non-college-trained agents, it is possible to find many who thoroughly enjoy their undercover assignments and are content to remain in that capacity indefinitely.

The Introduction

The initial referral that launches undercover agents on the road to infiltrating a criminal gang is of the utmost importance. In the classic book *Counterfeiting*, Lawrence D. Smith (1944) states that the agent must be introduced properly and under acceptable auspices to members of the criminal gang. The introduction must have the complete confidence of the higher-ups, and even so, criminals will still be suspicious of the agent at first. The agent must be prepared to repel that suspicion.

Carmine J. Motto, the author of *Undercover* (1971), also gives extensive support to the introduction as it was outlined by Smith in his book.

Let's return to Case 6 for a simple but classic example of how an undercover agent might obtain an introduction.

CASE 6: PEORIA, ILLINOIS (CONTINUED)

The undercover agent had been employed at the target business for several months and had devoted his activities to gaining the confidence of his fellow employees. One day at quitting time, he was approached by an employee whom he considered to be a suspect in the case. The employee invited him to stop off for a few beers on the way home from work. The men stopped at a local tavern in the city's warehouse district. The tavern was known to be frequented by professional criminals, and it was immediately evident that the employee was well known to the bartender on duty.

Initially, the employee made no introduction except to say to the bartender, "This is Harry." When it was time to leave the tavern, the real introduction took place. The employee called the bartender over to where the two men were sitting and told him, "I want you to know that Harry is OK." With this one sentence, the introduction was made. It was sufficient to reassure the bartender about the agent's future presence in the tavern. The various illegal acts that regularly took place in the tavern could continue even when the undercover agent was present.

The agent began to frequent the tavern on his off-hours, and he became aware that it was the center for a number of illegal activities, including prostitution, gambling, and narcotics. With the employee as a referral and the bartender to vouch for him, the agent was accepted, to a point, by the local criminals. They were willing to tolerate his presence during discussions of their activities, but to welcome him into their ranks would require better "credentials" than he had.

The Test

The "test" is an intentional move by the gang to determine the trustworthiness of their new or prospective member. It may come in the beginning or later in the case if suspicion arises from the gang. The common denominator of most "tests" is the commission of or assistance in some criminal act.

Motto (1971) points out that undercover agents are sometimes used as a courier as part of "the test" imposed by a criminal gang. Motto is quick to point out, however, that if agents accept an assignment as a courier, they should make sure that the receivers are aware of what is being delivered.

Let's look again at Case 6 to illustrate what the agent might expect in the way of a test.

CASE 6: PEORIA, ILLINOIS (CONTINUED)

One evening, the agent was invited to participate in a dice game in the back room of the tavern. He was asked to hang his jacket in the hallway before entering the back room. The agent was somewhat suspicious about the motive behind the invitation but later realized that both his coat and his automobile had been thoroughly searched while the game was in progress. The result of such a test would obviously be either the agent's further acceptance by the gang or his probable liquidation.

On another night in the tavern, the agent was present when a fight developed and a man was killed. The patrons did not call the police for a half hour, nor did they render any help to the fatally wounded man. Although it was contrary to anything he had ever been taught, the undercover operative had no alternative but to remain seated in the tavern until the bartender gave the sign that the police should be called. Following this incident, the operative was invited to join a highly organized burglary gang.

> AT THIS POINT, THE AGENT WAS HEADED INTO A COL-
> LATERAL INVESTIGATION (ONE THAT IS NOT DIRECTLY RE-
> LATED TO THE MAIN ASSIGNMENT AND HAS LITTLE OR
> NO BENEFIT FOR THE COMPANY).

At this point, a high-level contact was made with the mayor and, through him, with the chief of police. The undercover agent was given the green light to join the burglary gang and to participate in several burglaries while reporting confidentially to the mayor's office. Through his efforts, a trap was sprung on the gang during a burglary on a night when the undercover agent was not present. This came at the end of the investigation, when the agent was in the process of being transferred to another city. He did not need to appear in court and testify.

In industrial undercover work, the test sometimes consists of nothing more than a dare to steal company property. Most industrial undercover agents do not hesitate to meet such a weak challenge. These rather amateur attempts at a test can be contrasted with the far more grim situation described in the following case.

CASE 8: COVINGTON COUNTY, ALABAMA

The agent was unable to secure employment at the target company and so attempted to make contact with the thieves by another route. He obtained employment as a driver at a local taxicab company, hoping that it would put him in contact with the less desirable elements of the community and give him the opportunity to meet the suspected employees of the local plant.

> AN APPROACH OF THIS TYPE, KNOWN AS AN OUT-SIDE UNDERCOVER INVESTIGATION, IS FAR MORE EXPENSIVE THAN INFILTRATING SUSPECTED EMPLOYEE GROUPS FROM THE INSIDE.

During the time of the agent's employment as a taxicab driver, there was an attempted kidnapping of a local bank official's wife in connection with a bank robbery attempt. The kidnapping and robbery did not come off as planned but did result in extensive FBI surveillance of certain key members of the local underworld for a period of weeks. The new taxicab driver was suspected of being an FBI "plant." One night, the local gunman for the gang that operated the taxicab company took the agent into a back alley and placed a gun against his head. A confederate thoroughly searched the agent and his billfold, but fortunately no incriminating identification was discovered. The only identification papers in the agent's wallet reflected his background as a merchant seaman, which had been part of his cover story.

AS THIS CASE MAKES CLEAR, UNDERCOVER AGENTS
MUST NEVER CARRY INCRIMINATING IDENTIFICATION.
THE AGENT IN THIS CASE STUCK CLOSELY TO HIS COVER
STORY.

Following this incident, the agent was put to several
other tests, which consisted of transporting illegal whiskey in
his taxicab. The agent apparently passed all tests to satisfaction, and was once again accepted in good standing by his
crooked associates at the taxicab company.

Joining the Criminal Gang

Undercover investigators should not be reluctant to pass up the
first invitation to join in criminal activity. The invitation can be declined in such a way as to provide opportunities in the future. This
gives the operative's superiors the chance to determine whether
the operative's membership in the criminal gang will serve some
useful purpose for the company or for the company's relations
with the community.

If the operative accepts the invitation to join the gang, the safeguards protecting the operative must be even more stringent than
would ordinarily apply. Each situation must be judged on its own
merits regarding who should be contacted to set up the arrangement. Without complete cooperation and trust between law enforcement and the company security department, injury or death to
the operative or irreversible damage to the case itself could result.

NOTE

1. Under the Employee Polygraph Protection Act (EPPA) of
   1988, it is possible to give a polygraph test in circumstances
   such as these, assuming that the suspect is willing to cooperate and the procedures described in the act are followed.

6

Roping

Roping is the art of gaining a suspect's confidence to the extent that he or she will disclose prior, current, or planned criminal acts. *Roping* is an old police term that is seldom used today. Although admittedly old-fashioned, *roping* is still the best term to describe that unique talent that most operatives possess or develop during their career. Of all of the things that undercover agents do, probably the best mark of their success in the field is their ability to rope. Without the ability to rope, the agent's other talents are meaningless.

Do not confuse the art of roping with entrapment. This chapter and the following one present a wealth of material to help you make the distinction.

DEDUCTIVE VERSUS INDUCTIVE REASONING

Before proceeding with the discussion of roping, it is important to explore the differences between deductive reasoning and inductive reasoning. Deductive reasoning is the process of investigation that most police detectives and other investigators use. By uncovering facts about an incident that has occurred, the detective follows the direction of the evidence and arrives at a logical suspect. The detective deduces the solution to the case from the facts gathered.

Inductive reasoning is just the opposite. Through inductive reasoning, undercover operatives start with a suspect and look for the facts or evidence to fit their beliefs. All good operatives have this ability to some degree. Inductive reasoning gives operatives who are good at roping a distinct advantage over other investigators.

To illustrate the concept of inductive reasoning, consider the following examples:

1. Customs agents who work at airports process hundreds of travelers per shift. Because it is impossible to search everyone's luggage, agents must be selective in order to find contraband and make cases. They rely on a "sixth sense" to decide whom they should investigate. They try to be attuned to the "signals" that smugglers send. This is inductive reasoning.[1]

2. Store detectives who are good at their job have also developed the "sixth sense." A good store detective can observe the entrance of the store and pick out many of the shoplifters as they enter. The shoplifters unconsciously send signals that the store detective receives—inductive reasoning in action.

3. Years ago, old-time narcotics detectives could cruise the streets at night and spot drug dealers. It used to be common practice to stop suspected dealers and search them for narcotics. Detectives did not like to make such stops unless they believed that the dealer was "heavy" (carrying narcotics). Inductive reasoning took over and helped the detective decide whether to stop and frisk a suspect.

4. The final example of inductive reasoning is from the author's own experience. It took place after a "bust" that involved widespread theft in an Eastern warehouse. A young man who had worked for the company for only three weeks related his experiences. He was a

dock worker who had become involved in systematic theft with an outside driver. He explained it by saying, "It was about my third day on the job when Mike [the driver] came up on the dock. He looked at me and I looked at him, and we both knew we could make a deal." No words were exchanged. None needed to be. Each man had sized up the other as a crook, using inductive reasoning.

THE ART OF ROPING

When using inductive reasoning, undercover agents first identify the suspects, then use their roping ability to make the case. Looking at roping from the standpoint of an undercover agent engaged in law enforcement activities, Lawrence Smith (1944) makes the following points:

1. Undercover is a dangerous activity for the agent, and consequently, the agent must be able to identify completely with the criminal.
2. The more unsavory the agent appears in character and background, the more likely it is that the agent will be successful in roping.
3. The undercover agent must be a consummate actor. The agent's life may depend on his or her acting ability.
4. The agent must have the argot of local criminals and must mimic their mannerisms, their method of thinking, and their mode of dress. If possible, the agent should physically resemble the type of criminal he or she is attempting to rope.
5. When the occasion demands, the agent must be prepared to be arrested with the suspect and, if necessary, to do time with the suspect in a penal institution.

The following case illustrates this last point.

CASE 9: MINNEAPOLIS, MINNESOTA

At the time of the "bust," both the agent and one of the chief suspects had been apprehended by company security officers in the act of removing merchandise from a drug warehouse. Because both parties had been apprehended while in possession of contraband, the agent "confessed." Shortly thereafter, so did the suspect. Based on information that the agent had previously supplied, security officials believed that the suspect had concealed a considerable amount of contraband at some unknown location. Even though he confessed his guilt for the current crime, the suspect would not acknowledge other thefts or provide the whereabouts of the additional merchandise.

The suspect was arrested, charged with grand larceny, and placed in the city jail awaiting arraignment. Shortly thereafter, the agent was also "arrested," and arrangements were made to incarcerate him in the same cell as the suspect. When establishing his cover, the agent had claimed that he was from Michigan and that there were warrants out for his arrest. Based on this, it was easy for local jail officials and the agent to convince the suspect that he was being held on the more serious charge of being a fugitive and was simply awaiting his return to Michigan. During the next 24 hours, the two men confided in each other about their backgrounds. The suspect eventually revealed to the agent the location of an old garage where the stolen merchandise was stored. With this information, it was a relatively easy matter to obtain a search warrant and to recover the stolen property (Figure 6.1).

In industrial undercover work, the art of roping is based on the old adage, "It takes a thief to catch a thief." Naturally, this does not imply that an undercover operative should immediately plunge into criminal activities. To do so would turn away not only the honest employees, but also the hardcore thieves, who would view the agent as extremely reckless and a possible danger to their own welfare. Experience has shown that undercover agents who try this approach are given a wide berth and generally produce few or no results. The undercover operative must begin with more subtle activities.

Figure 6.1. Merchandise recovered in Case 9. A lunch box was used to remove contraband each day from the warehouse. The whole operation was exposed by an undercover investigator.

Roping Techniques

The following example illustrates how the process of roping might be gently developed. Imagine that a newly assigned agent is working on a production line alongside a number of other employees. The agent notices a manager entering the production area. He nudges a fellow worker and remarks, "Watch it! Here comes the boss." With this simple act, the agent establishes himself as being on the side of his fellow worker and opposite management. This is the first step in the act of roping.

Another helpful approach to roping is establishing a "criminal" background. For law enforcement agencies that suspect that their criminal records files are accessible to the underworld, it is a simple matter to "plant" fingerprints, mug shots, and an arrest record for an undercover agent. The fabricated record should generally conform to the type of criminal activity involved in the undercover assignment. It might even be desirable to arrange for the apparent arrest of the agent on minor charges to establish him or her as a criminal character.

Some successful industrial undercover agents use fake news clippings about previous arrests to help attract dishonest co-workers. A favorite trick is for agents to "lose" their wallet, containing a fake news clipping, in the rest room or some other appropriate place. Human nature being what it is, the average worker usually yields to curiosity. Not only is the agent's fake identification established, but also the agent's "criminal" background. Another trick is to "drop" revealing documents, such as a civil summons in a lawsuit, a notice of foreclosure, a repossession warning, a final demand for payment, or a parole or probation officer's business card. Use your imagination to devise similar gimmicks to assist in roping.

Let's return to Case 9 for an illustration of another roping technique. This technique is appropriate after the agent has spent some time on the job and developed strong friendships.

CASE 9: MINNEAPOLIS, MINNESOTA (CONTINUED)

One evening in a tavern near the plant, the undercover operative encountered a fellow employee whom he considered to be a theft suspect. The operative had no evidence against the employee, except that generated by his "sixth sense." After some drinking at the bar, the agent began to feign intoxication. He confided in the employee that he was a fugitive from a nearby state where he was wanted for a series of larcenies and burglaries.

THIS EXAMPLE IS REALLY NO DIFFERENT FROM THE "STORIES" THAT PEOPLE TELL EACH OTHER AFTER A DAY OF HUNTING OR FISHING. FACILITATED BY ALCOHOL, EACH STORY BEGETS AN EVEN BIGGER STORY.

The operative swore the employee to secrecy but, in the process, went into some detail on one or two of the fictitious crimes that he had supposedly committed. With the assistance of the alcohol he had consumed, the employee felt obliged to brag about his own activities. He told the investigator that he had single-handedly committed two drugstore burglaries for which he had not been apprehended. Not even his wife knew of his activities. Such revelations must always be viewed with skepticism, but in this case, a check of police records indicated that the two stores in question had indeed been robbed and no one had been apprehended.

Eventually, the mutual trust that developed at the bar between the agent and the employee led to a further revelation about the theft of company merchandise. This revelation came a number of weeks later. The operative did not push the employee for information, knowing that it would all come in due time.

Another roping technique is to commit a criminal act, such as the theft of company goods. When initiating such actions, the operative must be extremely careful to observe two basic rules:

1. Do not try to be the most active thief in the plant. Rather, be content to be no higher than third in rank.
2. Simulate acts of theft without actually removing the goods from the plant. Initially, undercover operatives will not know which employees are honest and which are not, and they must ensure that they are not reported to management by an honest employee.

If the agent is reported to management, the informant obviously cannot be "trusted" and in all probability is not involved in criminal acts. Experience shows that thieves seldom turn in other employees. Not only is this against "the code," but it generates a lot of unnecessary attention on the thief.

In addition, the operative usually should not commit or even simulate a theft in front of only one employee. This generally proves to be a waste of time and effort on the part of the operative. The operative should ensure that any thefts committed or simulated are performed in the view of at least two employees. The goal is to establish a reputation with fellow workers as being dishonest. When a theft is performed in front of two other employees, the operative's actions will become the subject of a conversation between the two others. Once two employees have discussed the action between themselves, they do not hesitate to continue the discussion with other employees who were not present. On the other hand, if the theft is committed in the view of only one employee, the observer will probably say nothing to fellow employees.

If a corporation or security agency asks its operatives to do their roping by stealing company merchandise, adequate controls must be put into effect and followed. Without adequate controls, the temptation placed before undercover agents might prove to be too strong.

Undercover agents engaged in taking company property as part of a roping operation must keep an accurate log of all items taken, and these items must be returned to the supervisor at the conclusion of the case. Occasionally, it is desirable for undercover agents to use "stolen" merchandise, or they might wish to retain some of the merchandise for personal use. In this case, adequate arrangements should be made to pay for any company property that is not returned at the conclusion of the case.

A final roping technique is for agents to display casually items that they have supposedly stolen from the company. Agents might display an item of stolen property in their automobile so that fellow workers can see it. If agents invite fellow workers to their apartment for socializing, this opportunity can be used to display "stolen" items.

Roping Illustrations

One of the most artful jobs of roping, combined with a proper cover story and adequate staging, was performed by William J. Burns in an 1897 lynching investigation in Versailles, Indiana. An excerpt from a biography of Burns by Gene Caesar (1968) follows.[2]

A band of burglars had been terrorizing Ripley County—breaking into isolated farmhouses at night, torturing at least one elderly couple to learn where their valuables were, and committing "other heinous crimes," which meant they had molested some local women. Three suspects were captured—an elderly giant of a man named Lyle Levi, and two of his friends, Henry Schuter and William Jenkins. The Ripley County sheriff went after two more suspects, a pair of hoodlums named Andrews and Gordon, and was badly wounded in a gun battle with them. A group of armed citizens joined with deputies in running down the pair, while the sheriff lay wounded. The deputies who were guarding the jail blandly insisted afterward that they'd been helpless because their shotguns somehow had been unloaded that night, when men with handkerchiefs on their faces forced their way in, gunned down Levi, Schuter and Jenkins, then dragged out all five and strung them up.

Were any of the jail's prisoners spared? Burns wondered.

Just one, he was told, a boy named Kelly, who was now in the state reformatory. But no one had been able to learn anything from him. He had obviously been threatened and badly frightened, and it was quite possible that he had no useful information anyway. Burns turned to the young detective, Steve Connell, and told him his job would be to enter the reformatory as an inmate and find out if Kelly did know anything.

"I don't know if I can do it," Connell protested. "The reform school kids don't even shave yet."

"Then shave at night when no one's looking," Burns said.

Deputy Marshall Ed Smith was a tall, rawboned Missourian in his mid 50's. Burns decided that he should go into the farm-equipment business. From his private-detective days, Burns knew a Chicago manufacturer he was certain would do him the favor, at least temporarily, of establishing a new outlet in Ripley County. Farmers habitually liked to pass the time of day in machinery salesrooms, as well as in general stores. With no women around in the salesroom, they talked more freely.

"A stranger opening a store in Versailles would create suspicion right now," he told Smith as they studied a map of the county. "Suppose you set up in the next town to the north—Osgood."

HERE, BURNS HAS DECIDED ON AN EXCELLENT COVER FOR HIS CO-INVESTIGATOR.

"When you hear anything worth passing on, don't take chances on any Ripley County post office. Drive all the way over to North Vernon in the next county to mail your reports."

BURNS HAS NOW SET UP PROPER LINES OF COMMUNICATION.

Now Burns began his own part in the strategy. Introducing himself as "W.J. Burton" at the Indianapolis office of the New York Life Insurance Company, he asked for a job as a salesman. He was curtly informed the firm had all the salesmen it needed, until he mentioned that he was willing to work the hinterlands on a commissions-only basis. Then a sales manager, who clearly regarded him as not yet bright, welcomed him heartily. So little insurance was being sold in the farm country that few salesmen were willing to waste time trying.

"What I would like to do first," Burns said, "is to learn the business as thoroughly as possible."

Not until he'd mastered every bit of information about life insurance the Indianapolis office had to offer did he go on the road.

BURNS HAS SET UP HIS OWN COVER STORY AND DONE THE PROPER BACKGROUND RESEARCH.

And even then he worked his way toward Versailles in slow stages, knocking on doors in one county while mailing his promotion literature to the next, polishing his role to perfection in safe territory and advertising himself well in advance. In dozens of general stores and taverns, in hundreds of farmhouse parlors, he played the part of a disillusioned traveling man who had grown sick of city life and hotels and restaurant meals and was longing for the earthy joys of rural and small-town existence. His reputation spread. If he was not always welcomed, he was always believed. Using county directories for his mailing lists and saturating every area with pamphlets before he entered it, he took several weeks to reach Ripley County—where practically every citizen knew by then that W.J. Burton of New York Life Insurance was coming. However suspicious the residents of the lynching area might be, none of them could accuse this particular stranger of attempting to sneak in. Burns' first stop in the county was Osgood. There, to the delight of lounging onlookers, he promptly tried to peddle a policy to the town's new farm-machinery dealer—a tall, laconic fellow who irritably insisted he needed no insurance and rapidly lost patience. The eager salesman persisted until a door was slammed in his face, and even then he insisted he was not discouraged.

"I'll sell that old mossback yet," he swore. "I'll be back."

He did come back—several times—as he solicited every possible prospect in the Osgood area. When he would return to the store and find no customers around, he picked up what information Deputy Marshal Smith had been able to gather from the talk he'd overheard. Smith was certain that men from all over the county—Osgood, Napoleon and Milan as well as Versailles—had been in on the lynching, and he had a few prime suspects to suggest. He'd also heard that the gun used to kill Lyle Levi was a .44 caliber revolver that had been borrowed from the window of McCoy's General Store in Osgood, then returned to the window, where it was still being offered for sale. But he didn't know who had taken the pistol.

All the answers, if they were to be found at all, seemed to be waiting ahead in Versailles. And Burns hired a boy with a wagon and an old white horse to drive him on down a dusty road that ran between fields of grain stubble and cut corn. The only hotel in Versailles was an ancient two-story building of whitewashed bricks on Main Street, with a tavern and a dining room on the first floor and sleeping rooms on the second. The hotel fronted on the courthouse square. Any newcomer stepping down from a wagon in that setting might have felt that the entire community was watching him from all sides. In the case of the alleged insurance salesman, this was more than just a feeling. When he went inside to register, he wasn't exactly welcomed.

"The town is right shy of strangers now," the hotel owner told him. "Might be best to move on."

Burns acted puzzled.

"Didn't you hear what happened here last month?" The man eyed him evenly.

Bill Burns shook his head.

"Well, some men were strung up, and if anybody ever deserved hanging, it was them. But there's been snoopers comin' around stirrin' up trouble ever since. So why don't you hire a rig over at the livery stable and get out of here fast?"

"I've already sent my firm's advertising to this area," Burns said. "I can't waste an entire mailing."

The hotel owner shrugged and gave him a room. From its window, Burns noticed that the white horse and wagon were still in front of the building, surrounded by a group of men who were obviously questioning the driver. But this was to be expected. Washing a thick layer of dust from his hair and face and brushing another from his suit, Burns went down to an evening meal.

He ate alone, and when he entered the tavern afterward, a hush came over the place. Hostile stares burned into him from every table. His attempts to make the sort of small talk he'd made everywhere else on his Indiana tour brought only muttered replies and turned heads.

Finally, a grizzled tobacco-chewing character walked over and sat down with him—a liveryman from the local stable and very probably, from what Ed Smith had overheard at Osgood, one of the lynch-mob leaders. Obviously delegated to question him, the man made little attempt at hiding his hard-eyed skepticism.

How much did an insurance salesman make a year? The liveryman wondered. How much on each policy? How many folks did he usually have to call on before he found one who would buy? How long had W.J. Burton been in the business?

AT THIS POINT BURNS IS ENCOUNTERING HIS FIRST "TEST."

Burns pretended to be delighted to find someone so interested in his work. He launched into a fact-and-figure-filled dissertation on insurance designed to dull the senses of any listener.

"You thinking of going into the business yourself?" he asked presently.

"Might be," the fellow allowed, tight-lipped above his tobacco-stained whiskers. "Might be doing just that."

Burns leaned closer. "Then why not list some likely prospects for me?" he suggested in a low, confidential voice. "If any of them buys a policy, you'll get a cut of the commission."

The man seemed taken aback by the notion. Muttering that he'd think it over, he got up and left.

Indiana nights had turned cold, but Burns left his window open when he went to bed. Shortly after midnight he was roused by soft but quarreling voices below.

"We can't take any chances," someone was arguing. "He was warned not to stop here."

"Anything more happens," another voice countered, "and they'll be calling out the militia or something."

Burns had a small pistol in his coat pocket. But at least some of the half-dozen or more men in the darkness below were probably also armed, and there was an entire hostile town to be awakened by any commotion. He could do little but listen, wait and hope. The muted debate went on and on, most of it in whispers he couldn't hear. At last the sound of footsteps faded down the sidewalk boards.

In the morning he began working Versailles much the same way he'd worked all the other towns, calling first on such prominent citizens as a lawyer, a banker and a real estate broker, none of whom wanted any insurance. When he returned to the hotel, he found that his room had been searched and his mail had been opened. But this too had been expected. The belongings he'd left at the hotel were strictly those of any insurance salesman, and his mail was solely from the Indianapolis office of New York Life.

He spent the next few days soliciting the merchants of the town. During that time, he later discovered, there were inquiries about him with his insurance company. Moreover, some Versailles citizens evidently hired a real insurance salesman to check out Burns because another stranger showed up at the hotel one day. Introducing himself as being in the same business, he then spent the entire evening doing nothing but talking shop with Burns, vanishing in the morning without any attempt to sell a policy.

THIS WAS A CONTINUATION OF THE "TEST," BUT THIS TIME WAS MORE THOROUGH. OBVIOUSLY, BURNS' COVER WAS HOLDING UP, AND HIS RESEARCH WAS PAYING OFF.

When Burns began calling on the outlying farmers of the area, he hired the very liveryman who had questioned him the first night to take him around. Outlining a route west of Versailles, he mentioned that he wanted to swing north to Osgood later in the day. "There's an old hardhead running a machinery store there," he explained, "and I'm going to write a policy on him if it's the last thing I do."

He found Deputy Marshal Smith alone that day, but Smith couldn't add anything new. On the way back to Versailles, Burns noticed that the driver seemed to have something on his mind. Several times, the scowling, bearded man turned and seemed on the verge of saying something, but each time, he turned back to stare ahead in sullen silence. The town was in sight before he finally spoke up.

"Did you really mean it about cutting me in on the commissions if I gave you some tips?"

For the rest of Burns' stay in Ripley County, the liveryman had a steady stream of suggestions to offer—most of which were still in alphabetical order, having been copied directly from the county directory. And Bill Burns could sense Versailles slowly relaxing around him. He no longer caused a hush when he entered the tavern in the evening. By the end of his first week at the hotel, he was being invited to eat with the owner and his family. Then he even began to hear fragments of talk about the lynching.

He showed as much curiosity as he estimated any insurance salesman would show, no more and no less. Gradually, he learned how the Ripley County sheriff, although still stiff from his wound, had actually been back on his feet by the night of the lynching but had obligingly stayed in bed during the festivities.

He learned how the five deputies assigned to guard the jail had indeed found their shotguns unloaded, having unloaded them themselves. At the end of about two weeks, Bill Burns had been accepted to such an extent that, when he mentioned he intended cutting a piece of bark from the hanging tree at Gordon's Leap, he was offered other souvenirs: one of the ropes used in the lynching and a handkerchief that had served as a mask.

PRESUMABLY, BURNS PRESERVED THIS PHYSICAL EVIDENCE FOR LATER USE IN COURT.

When he finally said he had to leave—protesting, truthfully enough, that he hadn't sold enough insurance to justify a small fraction of the time he'd spent in the town—the new friends this genial fellow had made were genuinely sorry to see him go. At about the same time, a Chicago farm-machinery manufacturer decided to discontinue a recently-established Osgood outlet. And at the state reformatory, an inmate who seemed older than the rest was suddenly released. Meeting at Indianapolis, Burns, Smith and Connell combined their findings into a detailed report that identified all of the ringleaders of the lynch mob, a good share of its members and even some of the onlookers.

Occasionally, undercover agents find themselves in seemingly impossible situations when attempting to rope a suspect. Imagination and inventiveness can often overcome what might otherwise seem to be an insurmountable obstacle to a successful undercover investigation. This point is illustrated in the following case.

CASE 10: LONG ISLAND CITY, NEW YORK

An undercover agent was assigned to penetrate a suspected group of thieves employed as warehouse workers at a wholesale liquor distributor. Not only was the warehouse organized by a labor union in a closed shop, but all new hires were referred to the company by the local hiring hall, which was operated by the union. In fact, the warehouse superintendent doubled as the shop steward. It was known that this union local was controlled by members of one of New York City's organized crime families. The waiting list at the hiring hall was quite long, and even the offer of a gratuity to the dispatcher could not guarantee immediate placement at the target location.

Using an entirely different tack, the agent and his superiors approached the head of the local security agency that furnished uniformed guard service to the warehouse. Normally, the tour of duty ran from approximately 8 P.M. to 4 A.M., and the guard's chief responsibility was to prevent local neighborhood youths and others from entering through the shipping doors and obtaining bottles of whiskey in a "grab-and-run" operation. The guard also observed the warehouse workers as they departed at 4 A.M. and made a physical inspection of their lunch boxes or other containers.

With the cooperation of the head of the security agency, the undercover agent was assigned to the local as a uniformed armed guard. As such, he represented to the warehouse workers law and order and management's interest. The agent's task seemed formidable indeed.

The agent quickly established himself in the eyes of the warehouse workers as a guard who was more interested in horse races and taking an occasional drink than in preventing theft.

IN THIS CASE, ROPING WAS AN ABSOLUTE MUST. IT REQUIRED CONSIDERABLE TALENT ON THE PART OF THE AGENT.

Eventually, certain members of the warehouse group began to offer the agent a drink on the job. The agent made a point of informing the warehouse workers that he would be forced to conduct a thorough exit check at 4 A.M. because of an impending visit from his supervisor. A routine soon fell into place: The undercover agent performed no exit checks unless an agency supervisor was present at quitting time. Before long, the agent was invited to participate in the card and dice games that the warehouse workers held during their lunch and break periods. He became generally accepted by the group even though he never became a full member of the theft ring.

Eventually, the case was broken because certain key members of the warehouse crew had given bottles of whiskey to the guard from the warehouse stocks on various occasions. Of course, these bottles were preserved as evidence and were used as an interrogation wedge following the apprehension. Initial admissions based on these free gifts of whiskey ultimately led to more complete confessions and full disclosures of the ring's activities.

INVASION OF PRIVACY

In a recent case that has not yet been fully resolved, a charge of invasion of privacy was leveled against Kmart, one of the largest retailers in the United States. A lawsuit filed by 43 employees of the firm's Manteno, Illinois, distribution center charged that undercover investigators reported on their private lives and on their union views. The employees discovered the undercover operation in progress during a vote to unionize the distribution center. The suit was filed under the Illinois privacy law. At least one of the plaintiffs stated that he had accepted an offer of an after-work beer from the undercover operative, who later visited the plaintiff's apartment.

The American Civil Liberties Union and various security experts concede that undercover agents might learn things that are not relevant to the investigation. The act of roping, which is essential for many cases, ensures that this extenuating information will crop up. Many observers believe that Kmart did not set out to spy on unions and did not do so, even inadvertently. Some feel that the suit was filed to generate support for the passage of the Privacy for Consumers and Workers bill (HR1900/S 984). At any rate, Kmart was successful in having the suit dismissed in Cook County Circuit Court.

At this writing, there are reports that the teamsters' union has taken a different tack following the dismissal. The union has filed an unfair labor practices action against Kmart with the National Labor Relations Board (NLRB). Final resolution will probably be a long time coming. In matters of this type, the NLRB frequently rules against companies, but then most of these decisions are overturned upon appeal.

The moral of this case is that when irrelevant information is uncovered during roping, undercover operatives are well advised to disregard and not report it. Labor spying is outlawed under the Wagner Act, passed in 1935, which established most basic union rights. By making their reports a model of professionalism, agents might avoid similar legal problems for their employer or client.

NOTES

1. It is true that customs agents now use a profile to identify likely smugglers, but the "sixth sense" was simply quantified to develop the profile.

2. Reprinted from Gene Caesar, *Incredible Detective* (Englewood Cliffs, N.J.: Prentice-Hall, 1968) with permission of Curtis Brown, Ltd., and Prentice-Hall, Inc.

7

Entrapment and Testimony

Entrapment can best be explained as the effort, on the part of the agent, to induce the suspect to do something illegal that he or she would ordinarily have no propensity to do.

As mentioned in Chapter 6, undercover agents must have a good grasp of the distinction between roping and entrapment. Failure to master this distinction leaves agents particularly vulnerable during cross-examination in court because the most common defense in cases involving undercover work is to raise the question of entrapment. Keep in mind that entrapment is not a crime, even though it is sometimes considered immoral or unethical. It is, however, a defense to a crime, and if entrapment can be successfully established during a legal proceeding, it is a sufficient defense.

Technically, only law enforcement agents can commit entrapment. From a practical standpoint, however, private security practitioners can also commit entrapment, which might result in the loss of a security discharge case being judged by a labor arbitrator. Moral considerations in nonunion establishments aside, labor arbitrators traditionally rule against management when they believe that entrapment occurred. Labor arbitrators are not bound by the rules of criminal law and procedure, and they run a much more informal proceeding. Hence, security managers must be alert to possible acts of entrapment on the part of their undercover operatives.

CONSENT

What constitutes a valid defense of entrapment to charges of larceny or similar crimes? Ronald A. Anderson, one of the foremost authorities in the field of criminal law, describes the general rule (1957). Entrapment occurs when the owner of the goods consents to its taking. In this case, the necessary ingredient of guilt on the part of the accused is lacking, and no crime has been committed. Interpretation of this rule rests on the distinction between active and passive inducement to the taking of the goods. If the owner of the goods or the owner's agent suggests the criminal plan and actively urges and assists the accused in taking the goods, this conduct is generally interpreted as a consent to the taking of the goods, and the criminal quality of the act is thus lacking. However, legal texts state that consent to the taking of the goods is not shown merely by proof that the owner or the owner's agent remained passive and made no effort to prevent the taking of the goods by the accused. It would also appear to be no defense to the crime that the owner or the owner's agent pretended to cooperate with the accused.

In the following case, a more technical form of entrapment—lack of want of consent—is indicated. As stated in the preceding paragraphs, if there is consent to the taking, then there is no crime. To have illegality there must be a "want" of consent. As legal authorities have always stated, a lack of "want of consent" amounts to consent.

CASE 11: THE BRONX, NEW YORK

During interrogation, the prime suspect in a theft case freely admitted that he had been supplying large amounts of pharmaceutical merchandise to a local druggist. The suspect, who was employed as a warehouse worker, described how he made deliveries to the drugstore about once a week. During each delivery, the druggist gave the suspect a list of requested pharmaceuticals for the next delivery. The suspect also revealed that he was due to deliver a supply of pharmaceuticals to the druggist at about 5 P.M. that day. The suspect had already gathered together the requested merchandise and had placed it near the dock doors.

Investigation officers immediately notified local police, and an elaborate raid on the drugstore was planned for that afternoon. With the permission of the security officers, the suspect retrieved the cache of merchandise at about 4:30 P.M. and took it to the drugstore. Security personnel watched as he entered the drugstore with the box of pharmaceuticals, which he carried into the back room after a signal from the proprietor. Local police and company security officers burst into the store and placed the druggist under arrest, charging him with receiving stolen property.

The case was ultimately thrown out of court on the grounds that the goods had not been stolen: The suspect removed the goods from the warehouse that day with the full cooperation and consent of the company security officers. Consequently, if the merchandise had not been stolen, no crime had been committed.

Although most states seem to acknowledge the general definition of entrapment, as described earlier, the courts in various jurisdictions are not uniform in applying the rule to specific cases. It is therefore difficult to fix standards for undercover operatives to follow to prevent the successful defense of entrapment. The majority view of the United States Supreme Court, as first expressed in *Sorrells* and reaffirmed in *United States v. Russell* (1973), is that the essential element of the defense of entrapment is the defendant's predisposition to commit the crime.

INTENT

In cases in which undercover agents are trying to lay the basis for a criminal prosecution, they must avoid originating the crime or the criminal intent. For example, if an undercover agent asks another employee to steal an article, entrapment would probably be a successful defense against criminal charges.

How far can a private undercover agent go in roping a suspect? Although the final test of an agent's activities must be met in court, many lawyers feel that the general rule of entrapment permits the following conservative acts:

1. Assisting the suspect in the theft of goods if the theft is first suggested by the suspect, who requests the agent's assistance
2. Giving the suspect opportunities to steal goods
3. Subtly suggesting knowledge of theft activities to induce the suspect to confide in the agent
4. Inquiring about methods of stealing goods in order to discover the suspect's *modus operandi* and to ascertain facts that will enable the agent to catch the suspect in the act of stealing

In addition to these four examples, there are probably a number of other cooperative activities that an undercover agent may perform to build a theft case, as long as the theft itself does not originate with the agent.

One factor to keep in mind when reviewing these guidelines is that they are all directed toward criminal prosecutions. Private companies should never dissuade undercover agents from breaking theft rings and uncovering dishonest employees, even when the agent's activities might subsequently rule out a successful criminal prosecution. Even when the rules of criminal evidence cannot be satisfied, an operative might be able to break a case, obtaining confessions and other facts that support the discharge of dishonest employees.

Company security efforts should not be confined primarily to conform to criminal rules of evidence. If this were the case, companies would not realize the full value of a security force, particularly in the prevention of losses through the early discovery of the activities of dishonest employees. A company's primary objective in any theft case should be the separation of the offender from the payroll. Successful prosecution should be only a secondary objective.

In addition, many aggressive law enforcement agencies do not seem to be too concerned with the rule of entrapment. Many successful undercover investigations probably skirt very close to a technical violation of the general rule.

Federal rules on entrapment, as they apply to private security agents, are reflected in the following extract from *United States v. Maddox.*[1]

> Briefly, the facts are these. Suspecting theft as the reason for its inordinate inventory losses, shirt manufacturer Alatex, Inc., solicited the private investigative services of its parent corporation, Cluett-Peabody, Inc., to locate the culprits. Cluett-Peabody's private agents, making known their desire to "deal" in stolen shirts, were contacted by the defendants and arranged to "fence" the merchandise in Atlanta. The delivery of 300 stolen shirts to the security agents sufficiently fulfilled the conspiratorial overt act. [1,2] (a) The defendants argue that the company's deep involvement in the conspiracy, to the extent of suggesting and arranging for the transportation, amounts to complicity and precludes their conviction because of entrapment as a matter of law. The argument overlooks the fact that private investigation, rather than governmental agents, participated in the arrangements. The entrapment defense does not extend to inducement by private citizens. United States v. Prieto-Olivas, 419 F.2d 149 (5th Cir. 1969); Pearson v. United States, 378 F.2d 555 (5th Cir. 1967). Moreover, the defendants received the benefit of the defense when the District Court submitted the issue of entrapment to the jury for factual determination. United States v. Groessel, 440 F.2d 602 (5th Cir. 1971). The jury found against the defendants. In any event, the conduct of the private investigators merely afforded opportunities and facilities for the commission of the offense, a continuing illegal enterprise, without initiating the criminal design in the defendants' minds. See United States v. Russell, 411 U.S. 423, 93 S.Ct. 1637, 26 L.Ed.2d 366 (1973).

Let's look briefly at two prominent cases that involved the entrapment contention: the Abscam and John DeLorean trials. In Abscam, several politicians were charged with accepting cash bribes. The U.S. government prevailed over the defense, which had claimed entrapment. (This case is discussed further in Chapter 1.)

The second case involved John DeLorean, a seemingly respectable automobile manufacturing executive who had formed his own company. He was arrested and charged with conspiracy to import cocaine into the United States, presumably as a way to raise money for his cash-starved business. The government's chief witness at the trial was a former drug dealer with a long criminal record. The defense claimed that DeLorean was entrapped by this former drug dealer, who was acting as an agent for the government. The U.S. prosecutor could not show that DeLorean was anything other than a respectable business man. He had no criminal record, and he had never even smoked marijuana, let alone dealt in hard narcotics like cocaine. The jury believed that entrapment had occurred and found DeLorean not guilty.

In conclusion, a good rule of thumb to follow in avoiding the complications of entrapment is to ensure that the idea of the crime originated with the suspect and that the agent's actions or suggestions did not cause the suspect to conceive of the criminal behavior.

WITNESS STAND TESTIMONY

In criminal court, labor arbitrations, and any other formal proceedings, defense attorneys will use every means at their disposal to discredit undercover agents and their testimony. They will attempt to draw admissions of entrapment or at least create sufficient doubt in the minds of the judge or jury about the legality of the agents' actions. For this reason, several helpful pointers on witness stand technique are included in this chapter. Refer to Floyd N. Heffron's book, *The Officer in the Courtroom* (1955) for exhaustive coverage of this area of courtroom testimony.

Appearance

When testifying in court, the appearance of undercover agents will likely differ somewhat from their appearance during the investigation. That is, agents should dress in appropriate clothing for the courtroom but not too different from their role as an agent, so as to seem credible to the jury. However, agents should not attempt to alter their appearance so drastically that they seem totally unlike the defendant. Agents must keep in mind that their testimony will undoubtedly relate to their roping of the defendant. Their ability to win the defendant's confidence must seem plausible to the judge or jury. A radically altered appearance during the trial might work against this objective.

Direct Testimony

In most cases, undercover agents' direct testimony will be narrative in form. Agents should give testimony in a clear and concise manner. They should never embellish or color testimony or betray any emotions of glee or disgust when describing the defendant's criminal activity.

Many successful undercover agents make it a standard practice to look toward the prosecutor when the questions call for very short answers. On the other hand, when asked to repeat in narrative form the details of the undercover assignment and roping activities, many agents turn slightly in the witness chair and face the jury when telling their story. In a trial without a jury, the same effect can be had by turning toward the judge or arbitrator.

Cross-examination

Many undercover agents, security people, and law enforcement officers make the mistake of becoming defensive when testimony switches from friendly questions by the prosecutor to unfriendly cross-examination by the defense counsel. Some people even seem slightly paranoid during cross-examination. These witnesses appear to be so guarded in their behavior that they seem to have something to hide. This, of course, is the worst possible impression that witnesses can create. Police officers who testify regularly are not as prone to become defensive as are private security agents who have less experience in court.

As stated earlier, the main thrust of the defense attorney's efforts is often to show entrapment by the agent. If no entrapment existed and if the agent wrote completely accurate daily reports, the agent should have no problem withstanding an attack of this type by the defense. The agent has already provided a narrative account during direct examination; during cross-examination, the agent need only stick to the facts previously stated.

In attempting to show entrapment, some defense attorneys try to create a doubt in the witness's mind of the legality of his or her acts and, in so doing, prompt the witness to alter previous testimony. The defense counsel might assume a posture of outward confidence of just discovering that the agent has committed an illegal act and is obviously unaware of it. This ploy is not troublesome to experienced agents, who usually know more about entrapment than the defense attorney, but this approach can be devastating to novice agents.

Along this same line is one of the oldest cross-examination tricks known. The undercover operative is asked if he or she discussed the case beforehand with the prosecutor or, if the proceeding is a labor arbitration, with the company attorney. An inexperienced agent might be tempted to deny this, thinking that the case should not have been discussed beforehand. If the agent denies any previous discussion of the case, the opposition will easily be able to discredit him or her. Note that there is absolutely nothing wrong with the agent's discussing the case with the prosecutor or even the agent's supervisor before testifying.

Another favorite defense approach is to attack the agent's lack of education or professional training. Many defense attorneys proceed on the assumption that undercover agents in industrial investigations lack training and competence. They will usually ask witnesses if they are familiar with the concept of entrapment. The questioning might then advance to some basic concepts of criminal investigations work, such as *corpus delicti*, chain of possession, and so forth. Well-trained agents have no problem with this type of approach.

In summary, undercover agents should remember that they are not entirely alone during the ordeal of cross-examination. If need be, help can be obtained from the prosecutor. When testifying, agents should make it a habit to pause slightly between the conclusion of the defense attorney's question and the response. This pause enables the prosecutor to raise an objection if appropriate. Once an objection is raised, it might be completely unnecessary for the agent to answer the question. Note, however, that many prosecutors are reluctant to raise too many objections because it might suggest that the agent has something to hide. Prosecutors occasionally allow a defense attorney to proceed slightly far afield, allowing the agent to respond to the defense attorney's challenges.

NOTE

1. *United States v. Maddox.* No. 73-2611, U.S. Court of Appeals, Fifth Circuit.

8

Supervision and Communications

In the author's experience of testifying in court as an expert witness on undercover matters, many cases have turned on the quality of supervision and communications. The very outcomes of some of these larger law suits have been determined by these points.

MANAGEMENT COMMUNICATIONS

In both law enforcement and industrial security, individuals who are privy to the investigation often tend to make supplemental communication efforts with the undercover agent. For example, a ranking police official or possibly even the commissioner of police might want briefings by the agent and might not be content to depend on normal communication channels. In industrial security, plant managers or company owners sometimes try to make direct contact with the undercover agent rather than wait for the written or verbal reports that the director of the investigation furnishes. These approaches are all highly dangerous and should be discouraged.

If someone of a higher rank must be taken into confidence to facilitate the undercover investigation, it should be made clear at the outset of the investigation that the agent will have only one contact (and possibly an alternate). No other contacts are necessary to review the progress of the case. Theories and other matters pertaining to the case must be properly developed before being presented in a written report.

Occasionally, members of top management or clients who are privy to the investigation believe that the agent should file more reports. Aside from satisfying the curiosity of the management personnel involved, more frequent report writing generally serves no useful purpose.

One of the biggest handicaps to a successful undercover investigation is the attempts of management to correct deficient situations within the plant or even to prevent additional thefts from taking place. This type of overreaction serves only to bring pressure on the agent and hampers the agent's ability to develop a solid case against the suspects.

Ground rules must be laid down at the beginning of an undercover investigation: Management must take no nonessential corrective action. If anything, management should ease off in disciplinary measures and corrective action to give the agent more freedom of movement and more opportunity to build a case. Private agency managers usually have more of a problem in this regard than their counterparts in a corporate security department. They can only counsel their clients and try to educate them about the proper posture during an undercover investigation. On the other hand, corporate security directors are usually in a position to cut off the flow of information to a particular executive if the executive begins to take unilateral action that hampers the investigation.

When planning to hire an outside agent, the security director or a representative should interview the operative that the agency proposes. The director should not hesitate to reject candidates until he or she is satisfied. Some directors have been known to place orders with a number of different vendors, believing that this increases the chances of finding the agent that can best do the job.

REPORT WRITING

Some private agencies require their undercover operatives to submit regular written reports. Other agencies allow their operatives to dictate the report via telephone to a stenographer or tape recorder. It is later transcribed, edited, and prepared for client review. Telephone dictation has inherent weaknesses from a legal standpoint: The final report is really a "rewrite" job, and the raw data is often not preserved as it should be. This procedure does have an advantage, however. It helps the agent maintain the security of his or her cover. There is a slight risk involved in the task of writing and mailing daily reports.

Law enforcement agencies are generally divided on the method of report writing to use, and much depends on the nature of the undercover assignment, the availability of secretarial help for transcription, and other factors. The major corporations and companies that use their own undercover staff almost always require written reports.

In addition to the obvious legal advantages of handwritten daily reports, the agents also tend to incorporate more detail in the report than they might during a hasty phone call from a public phone booth. The following case clearly illustrates the advantages of detailed written reports.

CASE 12: DETROIT, MICHIGAN

The agent had been assigned to a wholesale drug warehouse that had been experiencing heavy losses in prescription drugs and pharmaceuticals. After several months, the agent found that the local shop steward was responsible for the systematic daily removal of prescription drugs. The quantity involved, however, did not begin to account for the inventory variances that the company had noted during the last physical inventory. The agent faithfully made detailed reports each day but could make no further headway toward identifying other significant thieves.

From time to time, the manager of the investigation reviewed the agent's daily written reports. During one review, he noticed that on a number of occasions, two or three order pickers were observed removing empty boxes from the warehouse at quitting time. Apparently, these women had obtained permission from the warehouse supervisor to take the boxes home for personal use. They removed them, three or four at a time, telescoped together. It became obvious that the same employees were taking an unusual number of boxes.

SOMETIMES, EVEN SEEMINGLY INNOCENT ACTIONS PROVIDE THE KEY TO BREAKING A CASE. THE AGENT SHOULD NOT TAKE THEM FOR GRANTED AND SHOULD INCLUDE THEM IN THE DAILY REPORT.

On the suspicion that this practice might be the missing link in the case, the undercover agent was asked to pursue a friendship with one of the suspects. In time it was revealed that the women were part of a highly organized five-person theft ring operating in the warehouse. The suspects were stealing pharmaceuticals almost every day and were supplying various "customers" in the Detroit area with prescription drugs. The goods were concealed between the boxes that they had received official permission to remove from the building (Figure 8.1).

Most corporations with an in-house investigative department favor a style of writing that is quite similar to the style and format that most large service agencies use. Reports are written in the third person, and the undercover operative uses an identification number rather than his or her name. The reports can be mailed to

Figure 8.1. Security agents inspecting and inventorying stolen merchandise recovered in Case 12.

a post office box in a preaddressed envelope with an innocuous return address.

The reports should be written in such a manner that the agent cannot be identified if the reports inadvertently fall into the wrong hands. In industrial assignments, for example, agents should not describe their first day on the job by reporting all of the instructions and job orientation that they receive. If a report of this type is intercepted, it could easily identify the agent. The personnel records would indicate which new employee was hired for that particular department on the day in question. Instead, agents should report their activities as if they were sitting on the sidelines and observing the indoctrination of the new employee, even referring to themselves by name. Of course, the report should not dwell extensively on the details of the indoctrination and job orientation, but rather should report the incident of a new hire as a routine matter. The director of the in-house security department can withhold this initial report. In this way, the first report that is released will appear to have been written by someone who has been on the job for some time.

Agency undercover operatives often believe that they must give clients something for their money. In the absence of theft or criminal activity, they sometimes fill their reports with insignificant facts already known to management, such as petty violations, rumors, and innuendo. This type of reporting tends to wear pretty thin with most security executives. Note, however, that *relevant* rumors should be reported, but they should be identified as rumors.

Many beginning undercover agents have some background in report writing, but others have not had sufficient training. Therefore, time must be devoted to the basic structure of the written report. Police or security report writing is comparable to journalism in many respects. Students should know how to apply journalism's "who, what, where, when, why, and how" to their reports:

Who: The agent should describe as fully as possible the suspects or witnesses. If the agent does not know their names, he or she should resort to physical description, time clock number, or nickname. Eventually, the agent will learn the person's full name or identity. When that happens, the agent should refer back to the original reports mentioning that person so that proper identification can be made.

What: The agent should describe as completely as possible the incident that took place.

Where: The agent should describe the location of the incident. If the agent is new on the job and does not know the name of the location, he or she should include references so that the exact location can later be pinpointed.

When: In addition to giving the day of the week, date, and year, the agent should also note the approximate time that the incident took place.

Why: The "why" should be used sparingly, as it really relates to motive. Most agents can only speculate as to why an incident took place. If the agent includes opinion in the report, it should be identified as speculation and nothing more.

How: This is really the *modus operandi* of the incident: the means by which the suspect perpetrated the act. The suspect's method might become very important, especially in litigation that takes place years after the incident. Without a sufficient written explanation of how the incident occurred, the agent might not remember two or three years later the method used in the criminal act.

As mentioned in Chapter 6, undercover operatives should never spy on lawful labor activities. Even when information of this type comes to the agent's attention, it should never be communicated in a written report. The only exception is criminal activity—or conspiracy to commit it—on the part of a union.

What follows is a sample report of an undercover operative's first day on the job. Note that the report is written in the third person and that it does not reveal the writer's true identity.

To: J. Kirk Barefoot
From: Operative #28
Re: Ajax Distribution Center—General Investigation

Fri., Mar. 26, 19XX

A new man called Joe was apparently hired and started to work today in the distribution center. It was observed that he was brought onto the floor by the operations manager, Jack Smith, and was introduced to several of the employees and also the foreman, Jim Brady. After the operations manager departed, Brady was overheard to tell the new employee, Joe, that there were a lot of fringe benefits to be had by working in a distribution center as long as he kept out of the way of Jack Smith.

The day was spent unloading a boxcar that had been spotted during the night by the railroad, and almost no contact was possible with other employees; therefore nothing further to report this date.

Respectfully submitted,
Operative #28

The case report that follows covers one week's activity. Certain identifying names have been deleted, but in all other respects, the report is completely authentic. It is typical of what an undercover agent might be able to develop in an operation that has extremely loose security controls and widespread theft.

To: J. Kirk Barefoot
From: Operative #15
Re: Manufacturing—General Investigation

Mon., Dec. 3, 19XX
Nothing significant to report this date.

Tues., Dec. 4, 19XX
Charlie D. stole two heavy-duty extension cords from the shipping department today. He stole them by carrying them out in his lunch bucket when he quit for the day.

Wed., Dec. 5, 19XX
Mark S. quit work this morning. He got another job somewhere in Tarboro. Operative talked to Mike G. at lunch today and Mike related a conversation he had had with another employee. Mike said that the cutting table spreads were worth several thousand dollars and that he would like to steal one if possible. He was talking to Willie from the piece goods department. Melton F. said he will definitely have enough shirts to move a load at Christmas, so operative is waiting for Melton to make his move.

Thurs., Dec. 6, 19XX
Mule showed the operative today how to steal small items from the plant by concealing them inside of pants legs. He said many employees steal by this method. Charlie D. stole a length of cloth today by carrying it out in his lunch bucket. He waited until 6:00 to carry it out. He usually doesn't conceal anything in his box until after 4:00, when most people have left for the day.

Fri., Dec. 7, 19XX
The operative today saw Don R., one of the drivers, carry out a DO-1 box that was given to him by Ben M. The box was sealed

tight at both ends. As soon as Don got the box, he deposited it in the cab of his truck and reentered the plant. Because of the condition of the box and Don's actions, the operative is sure that the box contained stolen clothing. The B/M working in the piece goods department is Earl H., a.k.a. "Willie." The operative mistakenly identified him as Willie S. He is still looking to steal some small bolts of cloth. Dallas and Murphy have stopped their loan business until after Christmas.

Sat., Dec. 8, 19XX
No work today.

Respectfully submitted,
   Operative #15

An undercover training program must contain sufficient examples and illustrations to show new agents what reports should contain. One of the by-products of industrial undercover investigations is collateral information that can later help management strengthen operating procedures. In addition to the more obvious breaches of security controls, many executives want reports to include violations of plant rules, examples of poor or incompetent supervision, safety violations, bad housekeeping, and so on. It is not unheard of for highly intelligent and experienced agents to be able to put their finger on production bottlenecks and even make major contributions to overall quality control. Efforts of this type can stop losses that might cost tens of thousands of dollars per year.

In industrial undercover work, there are days when the pressure of work precludes agents from developing any significant information. On such days, agents should simply record the date and state, "Nothing significant to report this date." To do otherwise is a waste of the investigator's time in trying to compose a meaningless report for the day and a waste of secretarial time in typing such a report. Agents should be instructed not to mail their report until something useful has developed on the job. In other words, the required frequency of reporting should not be longer than one week. In the event that something of significance can be reported, the agent can mail the report immediately. This type of policy relieves undercover agents from a great deal of unnecessary pressure.

MULTIPLE AGENTS

Earlier chapters mentioned the coordination of the undercover operative and an outside agent who "works the street." This contact is necessary. When multiple inside agents are assigned to a case, however, they should always operate on a need-to-know basis. Agent A should never be aware of the presence of Agent B, and vice versa. The exposure of an agent can result in threats or physical violence. These pressures can easily force the exposed agent into a bargaining posture if he or she is privy to the existence of a second or third agent. This approach to the use of multiple agents might require the editing of reports and more direction by the supervisor so that the agents are not pursing each other. Obviously, though, the prevention of multiple exposure is well worth the precautions taken.

DEBRIEFING

The security manager should hold periodic meetings to debrief the undercover operatives. The monotony of undercover work almost dictates that agents will fall into a rut from time to time. Not only must they be remotivated, but the security manager must be sure that their reports are absolutely factual, especially if the reports were transcribed. Agents are like everyone else: They have biases and prejudices and sometimes play favorites. These weaknesses must be guarded against, regardless of whether the operative is from an outside agency or the company's security department.

When the company security manager participates in debriefings with an outside agency's operative, the operative is considered to be an agent of both the outside agency and the company. To not participate in the direction of the case would leave the security manager open to a charge of negligence.

9

The Burn

Probably one of the most critical times for undercover operatives is when follow employees accuse them either directly or indirectly of being a company spy. This is known as *the burn*. From the standpoint of the investigation, the worst occurrence would be to have the undercover operative suspected by fellow employees but never accused. Until an accusation is made, the operative is never really aware of the suspicion and therefore cannot take steps to overcome it.

One newly assigned operative spent four to five months on his first case without developing much information. The case was eventually broken through another lead, and the undercover phase of the operation was analyzed to find out what had gone wrong. From statements made by the suspects under interrogation, it was learned that almost from his first day on the job, the undercover operative was suspected. He asked an unusual number of pointed questions about the operation of the plant and about his co-workers. Within several days, he was known to his fellow workers as the "Eye Spy." He never succeeded in becoming close to anyone, with the exception of one individual who, being ostracized by the rest of the group, was not taken into their confidence. The agent never knew that he was under suspicion. He was simply unproductive in his role.

HANDLING THE BURN

Once an accusation has been made, the undercover operative can try a number of responses to overcome the pressure generated by the suspicions of fellow employees. Some of these alternatives are based on the premise that the best defense is a good offense.

1. The operative should treat the first accusation as a joke and attempt to make a jocular remark in response. To react otherwise to the first accusation would be overly defensive.

2. Making the same type of accusation against the main perpetrator of the stories is another successful technique. In other words, accuse the accuser. This should be used if the first response is ineffective.

3. If the accusations continue primarily from one or two people, the agent's response should be escalated. The agent should become "fighting mad" at any allegation or even any innuendo of being a company spy. This is meant not only figuratively, but also literally if the occasion demands. In one case, an investigator was forced to take drastic measures in a secluded part of the warehouse with a particular individual who was attempting to portray him as a company spy. As a result of this encounter, the suspicion ceased, and no more statements of this type were made.

4. The fourth and probably most effective response is to have the operative increase his or her own theft activities. It is possible to cite many examples in which the first two steps were largely unproductive but an increase in theft activity seemed to confuse everyone and completely allay suspicions. Many suspects report during interrogation, "I always thought that John Doe was a company detective until I put him to the test to determine if he would

steal. When he did, then I became convinced that he was OK." Such reasoning, although completely illogical, seems to make sense to the average dishonest worker.

THE BURN AS A TEST

Some employees or groups of employees make it a habit to accuse all new co-workers of being a company spy. If the person reacts adversely and quits the job, then they feel they have made their point. On the other hand, if the new hire can withstand the pressure and overcome it, then perhaps he or she is not a spy. Let's return to Case 12 for an illustration of this point.

CASE 12: DETROIT, MICHIGAN (CONTINUED)

The agent had been assigned to the drug warehouse for about four weeks when he was suddenly accused by a fellow worker of being a company spy. On the following day, several other employees also made comments in the same vein. Both the investigator and his supervisor were completely shocked because they had taken every precaution with local management to ensure the secrecy of the operation. Although the agent had not been able to secure a job on his own, he had been hired without any undue attention, and only the two top local managers knew of his existence. The only logical conclusion at the time was that there had been a leak in the case, and out of concern for the agent's safety in the Detroit area, he was quietly removed from the case and reassigned.

Several months went by before another attempt was made to infiltrate the work force. The second agent was able to secure employment on his own initiative, without the help or even knowledge of management. After about one month on the job, the second agent was suddenly accused of being a company spy by the same people who had similarly accused the first agent. The agent reacted in accordance with his prior training by becoming indignant and accusing his accusers of the same. Because there was no possibility of a management leak, it was decided that the agent would attempt to gain the confidence of his accusers. This was accomplished through a steady program of roping in the form of theft of company merchandise. The employees eventually confided in the agent that for a number of years, it had been a common practice to accuse each new employee to judge his or her reaction. This standard defensive tactic had probably been successful on a number of occasions.

SIDE EFFECTS OF THE BURN

Sometimes, the agent's attempt to overcome an accusation can have a positive effect on the roping of other employees. The following case represents a rather bold approach to allay suspicion. The undercover agent's actions were fully discussed with and approved by the agent's superior.

CASE 13: NORTHUMBERLAND COUNTY, PENNSYLVANIA

The agent was assigned to infiltrate a company operation that had traditionally hired only local people who were well known to management. The local managers were not privy to the undercover investigation, and therefore, special means had to be devised to enable the agent to gain employment.

The agent gradually overcame the initial wariness on the part of the rank-and-file union members in the facility and started to develop strong personal relationships with various members of the work force. At the same time, the agent was aware that he was suspected by the facility manager, who considered him to be a company spy. The manager used whatever influence he had to try to plant this belief in the minds of other key people in the facility. Eventually, the agent realized that there was a certain amount of suspicion focused on him because of the plant manager's allegations.

After he became a member of the union, the agent tackled the problem head on and filed a grievance with the shop steward against the plant manager for constantly branding him as an undercover agent. With the shop steward's support, a first-step grievance procedure was held with the manager during which the agent point-blank accused him of creating problems by referring to him as a company spy. The manager denied the allegation, and the grievance procedure ended with nothing definitive being accomplished.

However, because of his direct attack on the manager, the agent suddenly found that most of the rank-and-file workers were drawn even closer to him than prior to the grievance procedure. From that point on, the manager generally kept his suspicions and beliefs to himself.

Undercover agents should realize that unless a blunder of some type was made or the proper guidelines were not followed, the suspicions directed toward them by fellow workers are just that—suspicions. As long as the accusers cannot confirm their suspicions, the agent can usually overcome them and complete the investigation successfully. Admittedly, this requires a lot of "cool" on the part of the agent. Not all security and law enforcement personnel possess the ability to overcome suspicions, but then, not all security and law enforcement personnel have the inherent ability to conduct a good undercover investigation. Without question, highly successful undercover work demands its own special breed of person.

10

Shopping Investigations and Surveillance

One way to keep up the morale of undercover agents is to give them specialized assignments interspersed with undercover jobs. These assignments might take the form of shopping investigations or surveillance. This chapter presents an overview of shopping and surveillance cases so that new security agents will not be completely inundated when first presented with these assignments. It is not the purpose of this text to develop the skills of shopping investigators or to perfect the art of surveillance. These can be accomplished only through actual street experience and on-the-job training.

SHOPPING INVESTIGATIONS[1]

The shopping investigation is a common form of street-type undercover investigation. Shopping investigators service primarily the retail store industry but may also be used in other types of establishments, such as restaurants, hotels, and bars. The following dis-

115

cussion focuses on shopping investigations directed toward the retail store industry.

A number of private agencies around the United States offer shopping investigations. In recent years, many of the larger retail companies have undertaken shopping investigations on an in-house basis.

Service versus Integrity Shopping

Shopping investigations can be divided into two types—service shopping and integrity shopping—but it is now common for these two types of investigations to be combined. The rationale behind shopping investigation is that it provides management with a tool to evaluate the type of service being rendered by salespeople (service shopping) and to test the honesty of the personnel themselves (integrity shopping). In recent years, many security chiefs have questioned the advisability of combining the two types of shopping evaluation into one investigation. They have come to the conclusion that integrity shopping is compromised or weakened to some extent when combined with service shopping. Investigators must concentrate so much on the quality of customer service that they are unable to devote sufficient attention to the techniques needed to ensure good integrity shopping. Furthermore, many shopping investigators are excellent at service shopping but are poor producers when it comes to integrity shopping.

Techniques for Integrity Shopping

Integrity shopping can be defined as creating an atmosphere in which a sales clerk will be likely to commit a dishonest act if he or she has the propensity to do so. This is not to be confused with entrapment. Integrity shopping gives thieving employees an opportunity to commit the same actions that they commit several times a day with legitimate customers. The techniques used by shopping crews are varied in their approach, but all have in common the fact that the questionable transaction can be identified by so-called tie-down sales that are properly recorded on the cash register by other members of the shopping investigation team. A tie-down sale is just another sale that can be identified later by reviewing the cash register tape.

A typical integrity shopping crew consists of two or three people. The best shopping crews are made up of full-time shoppers who have developed their act and are proficient at it. An alternative to a full-time shopping crew is a nucleus of at least one full-time shopper, supplemented by part-time shoppers. Part-time shoppers can be recruited from the ranks of homemakers who at one time or another worked as full-time shoppers.

The crew is usually directed by a lead shopper, or crew chief, who is responsible for dispensing the cash to make the purchases, transporting the team, and working out the routing and schedule. The crew chief also acts as a liaison with the principal in the agency office or with the retail security manager in the in-house investigation.

It is normally up to the agency supervisor or the retail security manager to make arrangements with the crew chief for storing the purchases while the target stores are being shopped. Ultimately, all merchandise is normally returned to the company for full credit, and this is usually handled through a high-ranking member of the store accounting staff. In this way, the rank-and-file sales personnel do not become aware that the merchandise has been returned for credit. Figures 10.1 and 10.2 are examples of the report forms used by agency and in-house shopping investigators.

SURVEILLANCE

All well-rounded private security operations require personnel with moving and stationary surveillance skills. Not only is surveillance often necessary to augment inside undercover operations, but it sometimes represents the only means of building a case against a suspect. Even in street-type undercover work in which the penetration of a certain location or the roping of a particular individual is indicated, surveillance is almost always a first step.

Date Feb 3-9, 1978 Unit	Opr.	Start	End	Out	Hours	Issue	Mdse.
Cashier MD	M.D.	600.00			18	200.00	189.92
End Mi.	B.O.				13	200.00	191.50
Begin Mi.	C.N.				18	200.00	160.65
Total Mi.							
Car Used						600.00	542.07

Store	M.D.	B.O.	C.N.	Entries	T	Total
Case #	4.65	12.99	8.75	26.39		
Feb. 3, 1978		3.25	16.89	14.14	6	6
Boyd's	18.25	21.79		40.04		
Clayton	22.90	38.03	19.64	80.57		80.57
Case #	19.95	8.29		28.24		
Feb. 4, 1978	16.75	28.76	16.84	62.35	5	11
Boyd's	13.99		22.50	36.49		
Crestwood	50.69	37.05	39.34	127.08		207.65
Case #	6.64		32.55	39.19		
Feb. 5, 1978	17.92		2.60	20.52	4	15
Boyd's	21.75			21.75		
Jamestown	46.31		35.15	81.46		289.11
Case #	17.95	36.06	16.22	70.23		
Feb. 7, 1978	18.92	19.99		38.91	6	21
Boyd's		15.50	19.75	35.25		
Northwest Plaza	36.87	71.55	35.97	144.39		433.50
Case #	8.75	16.95	2.45	28.15		
Feb. 8, 1978	3.50	27.92		31.42	5	26
Boyd's	13.85		16.99	30.84		
St. Clair	26.10	44.87	19.44	90.41		523.91

Figure 10.1. Sample cash and production control form for use in a shopping investigation. Properly completed, this form provides an accurate record of what has been spent in each store. It gives the hours worked by the members of the crew and accounts for the shopping money issued, spent, and returned.

Bal.	Sig.	$ On Hand A.M.		$ 200	Total Ent.	
10.08	mD	Additional $ 400				
8.50	BO	Total Start		$ 600	Total Tests 29	
39.35	eN				Per Diem	
		Total	Mdse. Spent	$542.07	Itemize Exp. — Reverse Side	
57.93		Balance Forward		$ 57.93		

Store					Entries	T	Total
Case #		2.89		7.82	10.71		
Feb. 9, 1978		4.16			4.16	3	29
Boyd's				3.29	3.29		
West County		7.05		11.11	18.16		542.01
Case #							
Case #							
Case #							

Moving Surveillance

With today's varied traffic conditions, the ability to conduct successful moving surveillance is an art. Good "tail" people must have the ability to perform successfully in all types of conditions, whether it means driving on an expressway, in downtown traffic, on an interstate highway, or on a rural country road. Only expert drivers can master the art of vehicular surveillance. The best tail

Firm _____ Store No _____	Case No _____
Address _____ City _____	State _____
	am
Date _____ Time _____ pm Opr _____	Report No _____

Name Number Letter _____	Reg loc/no: _____ Reg read: _____
Sex _____ Age _____	Other cust/oprs/sales people: _____
Height _____ Weight _____	PAYMENT MADE
Build _____	
Eyes _____ Nose _____	
Teeth _____	DESCRIPTION OF TRANSACTION
Complexion _____	
Hair color _____	
How combed _____	
Glasses _____	
Jewelry _____	
Other _____	

PAYMENT MADE

	$20	$10	$5	$1	50¢	25¢	10¢	5¢	1¢	
1. Pur										Trans No. ____
2. Pur										Trans No. ____

Figure 10.2. Sample shopping investigation report form.

people are often employed as operatives for private detective agencies that specialize in marital investigations. Some expert drivers can successfully tail a subject for weeks—even when the subject has been alerted in advance about the possibility of surveillance. Despite the evasive maneuvers that the subject who anticipates a

Salespersons Appearance:	
_____ Well groomed	
_____ Passible	
_____ Average	
_____ Unimpressive	
_____ Unkempt	
_____ Other	

Salespersons Attitude:			
_____ Enthusiastic			
_____ Pleasant	PURCHASES MADE		
_____ Routine			
_____ Indifferent			
_____ Antagonistic			
_____ Served promptly			
_____ Suggested other items			
_____ Offered a 'thank you'			
_____ Other			

surveillance might attempt, these surveillance agents are successful more often than not.

Novice investigators must be trained in the art of vehicular surveillance. In surveillance work, both the subject and the investigator might be "burned." Subjects are said to be burned when they suspect or become aware that they are under surveillance, even if they cannot pinpoint any particular agent. When the term is used in connection with an agent, it is synonymous with being "made," or identified, by the subject. When burned, the agent's usefulness on the assignment is at an end.

Subjects use many evasive tactics for throwing off a surveillance, and investigators use an equal number of tactics for reducing the chances of burning the subject. As many of these tactics as possible should be demonstrated to novice investigators. Their own imagination and experience at this type of work will further expand their abilities. Such training is not unlike the defensive driving course that the major automobile insurance companies teach. The scope of this text does not permit an extensive discussion of vehicular tactics. The discussion is confined to the general points that the director of a surveillance operation should keep in mind.

The Surveillance Vehicle and Equipment

Rental cars are generally considered to be the best choice for vehicle surveillance. For a surveillance involving more than one person per vehicle, a four-door sedan is preferable because it enables the passenger to move to the rear seat to present a different "picture" to the subject of the surveillance. The vehicle should be chosen carefully; it should not be conspicuous in color. When the surveillance runs a number of days, the car should be switched with the rental agency every day if possible. Some rental agencies are amenable to maintaining the weekly rental rate despite the daily changes, especially if full-sized sedans are being used.

Among the items kept in the surveillance vehicle should be changes of outer clothing, such as caps, hats, and a reversible jacket or topcoat. Surveillance cars should also contain a pair of good-quality binoculars and a movie or still camera equipped with a telephoto lens. A closed container for liquids is necessary for the relief of personal needs during a car surveillance that will run an indefinite number of hours. A newspaper should also be present in the vehicle to provide cover for the operative when parked and to cover the operative's camera work. A person who appears to be reading a newspaper in an automobile draws far less attention than someone who appears to be doing nothing except sitting.

Some federal and private agencies that use automobiles regularly for tail jobs make certain modifications in the automobiles' lights. They install interior switches that enable the driver to shut off the left or right headlight. These options add to the number of different pictures presented to the subject's rearview mirror. Interior lights can also be modified by taping down the spring buttons found in the door panels so that the lights do not come on when the doors are opened. The investigator should never remove the bulb from the interior dome light; the dome light must be kept in operating condition for reasons explained later.

Risks in Vehicular Surveillance

During training, new agents must learn when it is permissible to take chances and when it is not. Any successful automobile surveillance necessarily involves a certain amount of risk to passengers of the car, pedestrians, and other vehicles on the street. These risks are increased when it becomes necessary to violate traffic laws, such as running stop signs and red lights or driving at excessive speeds. On a long-term tailing assignment, it is desirable to minimize the taking of such risks, even though the chances of losing the subject are thereby increased. Maximum traffic violations are generally permissible only when the agent knows that the "buy" has occurred or is about to take place or that contraband is being transported to a specific location. Only in these cases is it extremely costly to lose the tail.

Multiple-Vehicle Surveillance

The most difficult car tails are those that involve subjects who own powerful automobiles and are high-speed drivers. The high-speed driver is already a hazard on the road, and for this reason surveillance directors must exercise their judgment when deciding how to tail the subject. To successfully tail a high-speed driver, multiple automobiles must be used—a minimum of two and possibly three or four—all with adequate radio communication. The strategy might involve several cars leapfrogging the subject, running on parallel streets, or a combination of strategies.

In attempting to determine the regular route of a high-speed driver, the security director might plan a number of days of surveillance, allowing the investigators to lose the subject's car each day, but gaining additional information on the subject's regular route.

Departments or agencies that are engaged in a lot of vehicular surveillance can use a device that is attached to the subject's vehicle and emits a radio signal. This device requires a receiver/direction finder in one of the tail vehicles. The small beeper device is easily planted on a target vehicle. It becomes extremely useful when visual contact with the vehicle has been lost.

Truck Tails

Generally speaking, truck tails are much easier than automobile tails, and in corporate security work, they are probably more prevalent. Because of their size and unusual markings, trucks are easier to keep in sight than automobiles.

One thing that investigators must be aware of is that truck drivers rely on their large sideview mirrors. When making a turn, the tail car should always make a much wider turn than normal to keep out of view of the driver. On the other hand, because sideview mirrors represent the truck driver's only means of viewing to the rear, they are also an advantage. There is a blind spot immediately behind the truck, out of view of both sideview mirrors. To take advantage of this blind spot, the investigator must tailgate the truck, and a high degree of driver skill is required to avoid an accident. However, in heavy downtown traffic, this technique often represents the only way to stay with the truck at various intersections and through traffic signals.

In corporate security work, most truck surveillances are of company trucks that make regular deliveries or pickups. Because these trucks generally follow a prescribed route, it is often possible to determine beforehand which stops the driver will make. The surveillance agent can make a dry run of the route in advance to study traffic conditions, special turns, bridges, and turnoffs. The dry run also provides an opportunity to spot various locations along the route that can be used to minimize the agent's exposure to a burn.

Burning the Subject

In both car and truck tails, one of the biggest problems that new agents must overcome is that of mental attitude. All surveillance agents have at sometime had the feeling that they have burned the subject. Experience has shown, however, that this suspicion is usually unfounded, and the subject is not aware of the tail. The director of a surveillance operation should keep this phenomenon in mind and try to temper the agent's mental attitude with a dose of reality.

As a rule, subjects who have been burned usually resort to seemingly pointless driving tactics to confirm the probability of a tail. When the subject appears to be driving illogically, the agent must drop the tail immediately. This action confuses the subject further because he or she will be unable to confirm the initial suspicion. If the tail is not dropped, the suspect's next logical maneuver is evasive driving tactics, which tend to lose the tail.

Foot Surveillance

In vehicular tails, the agent must constantly consider the picture presented to the subject's rearview mirror. In foot tails, in contrast, the agent is more concerned with keeping the subject in sight and using common sense to avoid a burn.

In a foot tail, the agent must be prepared for almost any contingency. The agent must carry ample change to buy a newspaper or magazine or to make a phone call when necessary. The agent will also need sufficient funds in case public transportation or a taxi is needed. Changes of appearance are also desirable for foot tails, probably even more so than in an automobile tail, because the agent is more exposed. A cap or collapsible hat, a reversible topcoat, and sunglasses or other eyeglasses can greatly aid the agent in maintaining the cover. Other disguises, such as false beards, mustaches, and wigs, generally should not be adopted unless the agent is an expert in their use and the items are realistic looking.

During foot surveillance in crowded areas, the agent should always keep the subject in sight and should attempt to remain closely behind. Beginning agents should be taught to pick a spot on the rear of the subject and concentrate on that spot when following. The agent can also use reflections in store windows to keep the subject in sight. However, agents should be aware that astute subjects who suspect a tail will use the same window angles and reflections to confirm their suspicions.

If there are few people in the area during the surveillance, the agent must drop back perhaps half a block or more. If the street is virtually deserted, the agent should tail the subject from the opposite side of the street and to the rear. If there are pedestrians around, the agent should try to use them as cover.

When two or more agents are working together on a surveillance, they should use hand signals to communicate. These signals should be worked out in advance so that everyone on the tail team is thoroughly familiar with this means of communication. Hand signals are usually preferable in close-up foot tails.

A newspaper is a must for foot tails. It can be used to emphasize hand signals and as a cover for the agent when observing the subject in a stationary position. A small hole in the newspaper will not be discernible from a distance, but it will give the agent an ample field of vision.

Suspicious subjects use a technique called *rounding*, which means making an abrupt U-turn and retracing one's steps, in an attempt to confirm the existence of a tail. When the subject employs this technique, the agent has little choice but to continue straight ahead, at least until the agent can turn a corner or enter a store. During a rounding operation—indeed, at all times during the surveillance—the agent should avoid making eye contact with the subject. Eye contact, more than anything else, tends to confirm the subject's suspicions about the tail.

When tailing the subject into a building with an elevator, the agent should attempt to get on the elevator with the subject. The standard technique is to exit the elevator one floor above the subject and then, using the stairs, determine which room the subject entered.

In *The Big Brother Game*, Scott R. French (1975) observes that if the subject enters a restaurant and does not try to leave by the rear door, the agent should be prepared to enter and sit down where he or she can observe the subject. If the subject suddenly boards a bus, the agent should make every effort to board the same bus. As French points out, the subject may leave the bus quickly before it departs in an attempt to induce the agent to jump off and thus blow the cover. This emphasizes the need for more than one agent on a tail. If possible, the agent should be backed up by an automobile surveillance. Agents should always have a point of contact in the event that they become lost or separated. There must be someone at a telephone who can relay messages and attempt to get the agents back together again. This is quite common in many tails, whether foot tails or vehicular tails, and is an absolute necessity if the case is of some importance.

The use of proper cover for a stationary foot surveillance, such as would be maintained during a buy, is only limited by the agent's imagination. The agent could take cover as a construction worker, street cleaner, taxicab driver, fisherman at dockside, or sidewalk distributor of leaflets, for example.

Stationary Surveillance

Hotel Surveillance

Hotel surveillances are probably among the most difficult to maintain successfully. Larger hotels offer the agent more cover, but they make it more difficult to locate the subject. Smaller hotels offer the agent little or no cover, but they make it easier to spot the subject.

If the subject is not known to the agents by sight, they must work with a photograph. If the subject's appearance has changed since the photo was taken, identification might be difficult.

Few first-class hotels cooperate in the surveillance of their guests. However, the director of surveillance might be able to use personal friendships and contacts to at least gain the passive cooperation of the hotel's security chief. In other words, the agents themselves will not be harassed by the hotel's security staff, but the hotel's staff will do nothing to aid the agents in their work.

On rare occasions, agents can rent a room directly across the hall from or next door to the subject's room. This makes the job much easier. The agents inside the hotel are in a position to watch the subject's comings and goings. With radio communication, they can pick up on the street surveillance at the hotel entrance. If they cannot gain access to a nearby room, the agents must resort to frequent trips past the subject's room, listening for sounds (or the lack thereof) from within the room, and plugging the door. *Plugging* the door means inserting a match, toothpick, thread, or other small, inconspicuous item in the doorjamb so that it will drop to the floor when the door is opened.

Business and Residence Surveillance

Setting up a surveillance in a business district is usually an easy matter. Even if parking is a problem, the initial point of contact can be handled by one agent on foot with radio communication to the backup surveillance team.

When a long-term stationary surveillance is desirable in a business district, it is often possible to rent a small store or unused office. Most rental agents will agree to the temporary rental of such a unit, especially if the transaction is handled in cash. In this situation, remember that the rental agent might need to show the premises for legitimate leasing. The surveillance agent's furnishings, therefore, should be kept to an absolute minimum.

In a residential neighborhood, the point of pickup for the surveillance team can be a problem. Not only are neighbors apt to become alarmed and call the police at the sight of a strange vehicle parked in a residential neighborhood, but they might cause rumors that eventually find their way to the suspect, alerting him or her to the surveillance.

If an automobile must be used for surveillance in a residential neighborhood, suspicion on the part of the neighbors should be expected. The surveillance director can attempt to divert the direction of that suspicion. For example, the common tendency is to suspect that the location being watched is in front of the surveillance vehicle, in the direction toward which the agents appear to be facing. A clever surveillance director can position the vehicle so that the agents are watching a pickup point to the rear through the use of sideview and rearview mirrors.

The best solution to residential surveillance is the use of a surveillance van or camper. After a day or two, a vehicle of this type parked in a residential neighborhood draws absolutely no attention. Most of the neighbors conclude that it belongs to a resident's visiting friends or relatives. The use of well-equipped surveillance vans has gained popularity in recent years, especially in corporate security departments. One large mail-order house with numerous retail outlets across the country is reported to have about 15 of these vehicles in use. Although vans are generally not desirable for moving surveillance, especially of automobiles, they seem to be the perfect cover for stationary surveillance. Campers easily serve the same purpose; their only drawback is that there is generally no direct means of access from the inside of the camper to the cabin of the truck.

Report Writing for Surveillance

The format used for report writing on a surveillance case is quite different from that used in an undercover assignment (see Chapter 8). In two-person car tails, the passenger, in addition to being the lookout and an additional pair of eyes for the driver, is charged with keeping the report. A typical surveillance report is basically a chronological log of the day's happenings. This log is somewhat more difficult to maintain during a foot tail because, obviously, the agents on the street cannot stop and make notations on paper while tailing the subject. Often, they must rely on their memories to construct a report of the day's events. A sample surveillance report follows.

TO: J. Kirk Barefoot
FROM: Operative #31
RE: Arrow, Atlanta—Special Investigation
Tues, June 3, 19XX

5:30 P.M. Operative secured vantage point in telephone booth across from subject's apartment house main entrance, 252 Park Avenue.

5:48 P.M. Subject arrived at residence driving 1979 Ford Mustang, license #261 MCY. Subject parked in the apartment house garage, then proceeded to his apartment.

6:18 P.M. Subject looked out his front window.

6:21 P.M. Subject came to main entrance of apartment house, looked around, and then returned to his apartment.

7:11 P.M. Lights in subject's apartment were turned on.

7:30 P.M. Eastside Market, located adjacent to subject's apartment house, closed for evening.

8:17 P.M. Lights in subject's apartment turned off.

8:19 P.M. Subject appeared at apartment house main entrance and proceeded west on Park Avenue on foot. Subject entered Gloria's liquor store. Operative secured vantage point across the street at bus stop.

8:35 P.M. Subject exited store, not carrying any parcels, and proceeded down Park Avenue to Rhone Street, where he entered the Big D jewelry store, located on the corner of Rhone and Park.

8:52 P.M. Subject exited store carrying one small package. Subject returned directly to his residence walking at a very fast pace.

8:54 P.M. Lights in subject's apartment turned on. Operative returned to previous vantage point.

9:47 P.M. Diamond Co. taxicab 406 arrived at subject's apartment house and immediately departed after letting its fare off.

10:08 P.M. Subject's apartment lights turned off.

11:00 P.M. Operative discontinued surveillance and returned to residence.

Respectfully submitted,
Operative #31

Coordinating with the Police

The question of whether and to what extent to bring the local police into a private investigation can be a thorny one. The problem arises because police patrols are bound to come into contact with stationary surveillance teams, or police officers might be dispatched in response to telephone complaints from neighbors.

When stopping surveillance agents, the police view them as suspicious persons who are loitering in the area. The officer might require the agents to get out of the vehicle and undergo a search. They might even call for an additional backup unit with the intention of taking the agents to police headquarters for further questioning. Such activity tends to attract the attention of neighbors and, of course, makes it impossible to use that location for surveillance again.

Under no circumstances should members of a surveillance team reveal to squad car personnel the target of their surveillance. It is normally sufficient for the agents to identify themselves and explain that they are on a surveillance but cannot reveal the target of the surveillance. In some small, rural communities, it might be advisable for investigators to present their driver's license and give some pretext for their presence rather than show official identification.

If the security executive decides that the local chief of police or another high-ranking police official can be trusted, he or she should try to work out an arrangement whereby members of the surveillance team would tell patrol officers, "We are on a special project with which Chief Jones is thoroughly familiar." This might not completely satisfy the patrol officer, but he or she will usually think twice before challenging the statement.

In a large police department, prior arrangements can sometimes be made so that patrol officers are informed that a surveillance car with private agents will be positioned in the area. The area so designated might not be the target of the surveillance itself but an adjoining block. Even if a certain amount of suspicion is created on the part of the local residents, it will not be apt to filter back to the suspect.

When agents are stopped by a police car for speeding, they will usually be allowed to proceed without a citation if they display proper credentials and explain to the officer that they are on a tail job involving a larceny or other crime. Again, the agents should not reveal the type of vehicle they are tailing; this information is not required. If an officer presses for additional information, it is only to satisfy personal curiosity.

If surveillance agents on a stationary stakeout of a location are approached at night by a police officer, their first act should be to turn on the car's interior light. Most police officers are extremely wary of approaching the occupants in a parked car at night. They usually do so only when they have unholstered their weapons or at least removed the safety snap from the holster. The appearance of an interior light in the automobile reduces the approaching officer's anxiety and conveys the message that the agents are legitimate and that the situation poses no undue risks.

Communication and Special Equipment

When coordinating with either inside or street undercover agents, the surveillance agents should work out in advance a contact through which messages can be relayed by telephone. If the undercover agent becomes aware of last-minute changes in the suspect's planning and a prearranged line of communication is not set up, the agent will be unable to convey this information to those on surveillance. The undercover agent might also need to identify certain suspects in the case. This, of course, must be worked out in advance with the surveillance personnel so that they can "pick up," or identify, the correct suspects. (In surveillance work, the term *pick up* should not be confused with its use as a synonym for *apprehend*. It denotes the beginning of a tail job of a particular subject at a specific location.)

Before the advent of modern radio equipment, hand signals were often the only way to accomplish the leapfrog multiple-vehicle surveillance technique. Today, nationwide companies can obtain designated wavelengths for the use of ultrahigh-frequency (UHF) radio equipment. A good radio communications consultant is the key to solving radio problems. One corporation was able to secure a radio license covering every major location in the United States within its industrial complex. This enables its corporate security department to move from locale to locale and still use its UHF radio equipment legally.

Earlier in this chapter, the use of specially equipped surveillance vans was discussed. Many security departments purchase stock vans from major auto manufacturers and modify them for their own surveillance use. If a surveillance van is to be disguised in some way, proper consideration should be given to the van's cover. For example, a sign on the van might advertise an industrial testing company, an engineering survey company, or a pollution study firm. If such a cover is used and signs are affixed to the van, the cover should be complete with telephone numbers for the fictitious company's answering service.

The interior of the van can be customized to meet the needs of the operation but should contain camera equipment, binoculars, a chemical toilet, and enough food and beverages to enable the agent to remain in the van for several days. A folding cot, a small table for writing reports, and other emergency equipment are required.

An innovation for surveillance vans is a type of periscope that enables the occupants of the van not only to observe their target, but also to use their camera equipment through the periscope. Lacking a periscope, the van can be rigged with blackout curtains on all windows except the one being used for observation. Special curtains of linen composition enable the occupant to view outward through a curtain, but it is virtually impossible for someone on the outside to see in.

NOTE

1. The remainder of this chapter was adapted from J. Kirk Barefoot, *Employee Theft Investigation,* 2d ed. (Boston: Butterworths, 1990).

Conclusion

In this book, I have tried to provide insight into some of the duties that newcomers to the security field will face in the position of undercover agent. The basic principles of undercover work should also prove helpful to police rookies and their supervisors.

Many top-level corporate security managers are reluctant to consider undercover investigations because of the poor experiences that they or others have had. It is hoped that by following closely the principles and examples presented in this book, they can avoid such untoward experiences in the future and make successful cases. Cost-benefit analyses often reveal how worthwhile undercover operations can be.

I have encountered many graduates of criminal justice and industrial security programs who feel that because of their educational background, they should be immediately eligible for junior management positions. They have no desire to work in entry-level security positions, such as undercover operative, surveillance agent, store detective, or guard. These young people should reflect further. In these positions, newcomers have the opportunity to be involved in the successful cases that mark the career of a top security executive. Furthermore, without experience in these positions, there is no way that a security executive can effectively teach these skills to others. Finally, the executive who has not engaged in these activities lacks a complete understanding of the security business.

I am proud that I have worked in all four of these positions during my career. They are absolutely essential to maintaining the momentum of a successful security program. Because I am familiar with the problems encountered by agents in these beginning assignments, I believe that I am a better leader and teacher than I would otherwise have been.

Bibliography

Ackerman, E.C. Mike. *Street Man*. New York: Writers Alliance, 1976.

Anderson, Ronald A. *Wharton's Criminal Law and Procedure*. Rochester, N.Y.: Rochester Lawyers Cooperative, 1957.

Astor, Saul D. "Undercover Investigation: A View from the Grass Roots." *Security World*, September 1969.

Barefoot, J. Kirk. *Employee Theft Investigation*, 2d ed. Boston: Butterworths, 1990.

Barefoot, J. Kirk. *The Polygraph Story*. Linthicum Heights, Md.: American Polygraph Association, 1974.

Caesar, Gene. *Incredible Detective*. Englewood Cliffs, N.J.: Prentice-Hall, 1968.

Carlson, John Roy. *Undercover*. New York: Dutton, 1943.

Cevetic, Matthew. *The Big Decision*. Los Angeles: 1959.

Donovan, James B. *Strangers on a Bridge*. London: Martin Seckler & Warburg, 1964.

French, Scott R. *The Big Brother Game*. Secaucus, N.J.: Lyle Stewart, 1975.

Greene, Robert W. *The Sting Man*. New York: Dutton, 1981.

Heffron, Floyd N. *The Officer in the Courtroom*. Springfield, Ill.: Thomas, 1955.

Hunt, Morton M. "Private Eye to Industry." *Harpers*, November 1961.

Johnson, James F., and Miller Floyd. *The Man Who Sold the Eiffel Tower*. Garden City, N.Y.: Doubleday, 1961.

Lubash, Arnold H. "Case of the Phony Gangster (Entrapment)." *New York Times*, February 4, 1973.

Motto, Carmine J. *Undercover*. Springfield, Ill.: Thomas, 1971.

Reynolds, E. Stanley. *Undercover Investigations Curtail Dishonesty*. Advance Industrial Security Information Service.

Schorr, Bert. "More Companies Hire Secret Agents to Spot Stealing, Malingering." *Wall Street Journal*, August 15, 1961.

Schultz, Donald O., and Loran A. Norton. *Police Operational Intelligence*. Springfield, Ill.: Thomas, 1968.

Smith, Lawrence D. *Counterfeiting*. New York: Norton, 1944.

Steven, Stewart. *The Spymasters of Israel*. New York: Macmillan, 1980.

Vizzini, Sal (with Oscar Fraley and Marshal Smith). *Vizzini*. Pinnacle Books/Arbor House, 1973.

Watson, Bob. "Critical Choices in Undercover Investigations." Paper delivered to the American Society for Industrial Security, at Annual Seminar, Nashville, TN, September, 1989.

Wesker, Rand S. "Stationary Surveillance." *Security Industry & Product News*, April 1981.

Index

Abel, Rudolph, 1–2
Abscam, 4, 93–94
Ackerman, Mike, 58–60
agencies, investigative
  local vs. national, 7
  private vs. in-house, 6–10
    cost comparison of, 7–8
  recruiting for, 14–15
agents
  college educated, 15–17, 63
  and criminal acts, 66–67, 73–74,
    77–78
  education level of, 15–17
  exposure of, 108, 109–113
  female, 54
  identities for, new, 28–29
  and morale, 63, 64–65, 108, 115
  multicultural, 14, 62
  multiple, 108
  payroll issues, 27–28, 55–56
  physical appearance of, 5, 14, 73
  and prior drug use, 42
  prior experience of, 15–16
  and realistic expectations,
    63–64
  recruiting, 13–17
  screening tests for, 17–18

Air Force
  Office of Special Investigations
    (OSI), 3
alcohol use, 63
American Civil Liberties Union, 87
amphetamines, 40
Anderson, Ronald A., 90
André, John, 1
antiespionage, 4
application process, employment,
  51–52
Army Security Agency (ASA), 4
Assignment, The, 71
athletic pools, 37

barbiturates, 40
Barefoot, J. Kirk & Associates, 22
bargaining units, right to representation, xiii
Big Brother Game, The (French), 127
Big Decision, The, 11n, 24, 25
bolita operations, 29
Boyd, Belle, 1
Burn, The, 109–113
  responses to, 110–111
  and surveillance 121–122, 125
  as test, 111–112

Burns Security Services, 7
Burns, William J., 79–85
business/industry investigations,
 5–10
  average case length, 10
  and criminal prosecution, 92–93
  and employee theft, 5–6
  in-house vs. outside investigators
  in, 6–10, 68
  and management invervention,
  100
  recruiting for, 15–17
  training in, 21–26
  use of undercover agents in, 20

cases
  Bridgeport, CT horse race
  betting, 37–38
  Bronx, NY entrapment, 90–91
  Cincinnati, OH female agent, 54
  Covington, AL infiltration, 68–69
  Detroit, MI burn, 111–112
  Detroit, MI report writing,
  101–102
  Jackson, MS staging, 58
  Long Island City, NY liquor
  larceny, 85–86
  Memphis, TN agent
  identification, 55
  Minneapolis, MN roping, 74,
  76–77
  Northumberland, PA burn,
  112–113
  Peoria, IL gang introduction,
  65–66
  Peoria, IL moving agent, 56–57
  Peoria, IL the test, 67
  Pittsburgh, PA larceny, 43–45
  Skokie, IL policy betting, 31, 37
Central Intelligence Agency (CIA),
 1–2, 4
Cevetic, Matthew, 1–2, 4, 10n–11n
 The Big Decision, 11n, 24, 25
clothes
  for court testimony, 94–95
  for cover, 52

Cluett, Peabody & Company, 22
cocaine, 40, 41
Cohen, Eli, 57
collateral investigations, 67
college trained investigators
  advantages/disadvantages of,
  16–17
  background of, 17
  and morale, 63, 64–65
  willingness to work undercover,
  17, 25
communication, 99–101. *See also*
  reports
  dangers in, 99–100
  radio, 123–124
consent, 90–91. *See also* entrapment
corpus delicti, 44
Counterfeiting (Smith), 65
Counter Intelligence Corps, 4
court testimony, 94–97
  clarity in, 95
  cross-examinations, 95–96
  and defensiveness, 95
  dressing for, 94–95
  and training, 21
cover stories, 47–60
  and appropriate dress, 52
  and banking, 55–56
  and credit, 52
  establishing criminal background
  in, 76–77
  and female agents, 54
  and household moves, 56–57
  and identification, 48, 55
  and local jobs, 47–48, 49–52
  and location, familiarity with,
  48–49
  staging, 57–60
  three "musts" for, 48
  time to develop, 49
credit, 52–53
  -reporting system, 53
criminal acts, by investigators
  and company merchandise, 78
  and entrapment, 92–94
  in roping, 73–74, 77–78

rules for, 77
as the "test," 66–67
traffic violations, 123, 132
criminal justice programs, 15–17. *See
also* college-trained investigators
criminal prosecution, as secondary
objective, 92–93
customs agents, 72

debriefing, 108
deductive reasoning, 71–73
DeLorean, John, 94
detectives, narcotics, 72
detectives, store, 72
Drug Enforcement Administration
(DEA), 11n, 39. See also Federal
Bureau of Narcotics
drugs, illegal, 38–42
dispensing of, 39
and evidence gathering, 41
legal considerations for agents,
41–42
most common, in businesses, 39
screening programs, 39
slang terms for, 40

Employee Polygraph Protection Act
(EPPA), 69n
employee theft
costs of, 5–6
exposing, 63–64
employment, as cover, 47–52
applying for, 51–52
getting hired for, 49–51
in staging, 58–60
entrapment. *See also* roping
and Abscam, 4, 93–94
and agent training, 21
and consent, 90–91
and court testimony, 96–97
as defense, 89–90
definition of, 89, 91
federal rules on, 93–94
and intent, 92–94
evidence
and agent training, 21

marking, 43–44
obtaining, 31–37
expense reports, 26

Federal Bureau of Investigation
(FBI), 2, 4
Financial Institution Fraud and
Failure statistics, 6
Federal Bureau of Narcotics, 5, 11n.
See also Drug Enforcement
Administration
Financial Institution Fraud and
Failure (FIF) statistics, 6
football cards, 35
foot surveillance, 125–127
appearance for, 125
in buildings, 126–127
communication in, 126
and eye contact, 126
French, Scott R., 127

gambling, 29–38
athletic pools, 37
bankrolls, 37
bolita operations, 29
football cards, 35
gathering evidence of, 31–37
local customs of, 29–30
numbers racket, 29, 30, 31
policy operations, 29
signs of, 30–31
and telephone use, 30

hashish, 40
Heffron, Floyd N., 94
heroin, 40
honesty, testing for
and integrity shopping, 116–117
and local employment, 52
prospective agents, 18
Hunt, Morton M., 48

identification
incriminating, 55, 69
local, 48–49
and new identities, 28–29

inductive reasoning, 72–73
infiltration
  of criminal gangs, 62–69
  introduction in, 65–66
  and joining, 69
  preparation for, 63–65
  of radical organizations, 3
  testing as part of, 66–69
  of the underworld, 61–62
  vs. outside investigation, 68
informants, 62
integrity shopping, 116–117
intent, 92–94. *See also* entrapment
interrogation, right to representation
  during, xiii
introduction, in infiltration, 65–66
Introduction, The, 75
invasion of privacy, 86–87
Investigation, Inc., 7

Kmart, 86–87

language, and roping, 73
larceny cases, 43–45
  proving, 44
law enforcement agencies
  coordinating surveillance with,
  131–132
  and outside agencies, 14
  and recruiting, 13–14
  rookie officers, 2–3
  undercover agents in, 2–3
lead numbers, 37. *See also* gambling
legal considerations. *See also*
  criminal act, by investigators
  in drug operations, 41–42
  traffic violations, 123, 132
Lincoln Controls, 7
LSD, 39, 40

Management Safeguards, 21
marijuana
  possession/use of, 41–42
  slang terms for, 40
  testing for, 39

marital investigations, 120
McKesson Corporation, 6, 9–10
  training program, 21–25
methaqualone, 40
military intelligence, 3–5
  history of, 1–2
morale, 63, 64–65, 108, 115
morphine, 40
Motto, Carmine J., 65, 66
moving, household, 56–57
multicultural considerations
  in infiltration, 62
  and recruiting, 14, 17

National Labor Relations Board
  (NLRB), 87
  v. J. Weingarten Inc., xiii–xiv
National Retail Federation, 6
National Security Agency (NSA), 4
Naval Investigations Services
  Organization (NISO), 3
negligence, 108
numbers racket, 29, 30, 31
  numbers slips, 32, 36

Officer in the Courtroom (Heffron), 94
Office of Special Investigations
  (OSI), 3

payroll
  checks, picking up, 27, 55–56
  costs, and training, 20–21
  and outside funds, 27–28
  records, 27, 28
  and witholding, 28–29
peyote, 40
phencyclidine, 40
Philbrick, Herbert A., 4, 11n
pick up, 132. *See also* surveillance
Pinkerton, Allan, 1, 10n
Pinkerton Detective Agency, Inc., 2,
  10n
policy operations, 29. *See also*
  gambling
polygraph examination, 69
  and prospective agents, 18

privacy, invasion of, 86–87
psychological profile test, 17

radical organizations, infiltrating, 3
radio equipment, 133
recruiting
    and in-house security, 15–17
    in law enforcement, 13–14
    in private agencies, 14–15
references, 51
Reid Report, 18
reports, 101–108
    and court testimony, 96
    and evidence marking, 43
    first, 103, 105–106
    frequency of, 100, 107–108
    information in, 104–105
    innocent actions in, 102, 104
    and invasion of privacy, 105
    risk in sending, 101
    samples of, 105–107
    and stolen merchandise, 78
    and surveillance, 129–130
    training, in writing, 24, 107
    writing style for, 102–105
retentive powers test, 18
roping, 71–88. *See also* entrapment
    and burn, overcoming, 112–113
    and college trained investiga-
tors, 17
    communication in, 80
    deductive/inductive reasoning in,
71–73
    definition of, 71
    illustrations of, 79–86
    importance of, 73
    and invasion of privacy, 86–87
    and irrelevant information, 87
    techniques, 75–78
    training in, 24–25
rounding, 126
runners, 30. *See also* gambling
Seckler, Frank, 9–10
self-employed, representing
    investigators as, 56

service shopping, 116
shopping investigations, 115–121
    forms used in, 118–121
    service vs. integrity shopping, 116
    techniques for, 116–117
Smith, Lawrence D., 65
Social Security Administration, 28–29
Spymasters of Israel, The, (Steven),
57
staging, 25, 57–60
    and local employment, 58–60
Steven, Stewart, 57
sting operations, 3
supervision, 99–108
    communication in, 99–101
    and debriefing, 108
    and multiple agents, 108
    and outside agents, 100–101
    and reports, 100, 101–108
surveillance, 117–133
    business/residence, 128–129
    communication/equipment for,
132–133
    contacts for, 132
    foot, 125–127
    hotel, 127–128
    moving, 119–127
    pick up, 132
    and police, 131–132
    reports for, 129–130
    risks in, 123
    and rounding, 126
    stationary, 127–129
    vehicles for, 122–123, 129

Test, The, 76
tests
    burn as, 111–112
    and infiltration, 66–69, 82–83
    and local employment, 50, 51–52
    for prospective agents, 17–18
tie-down sales, 116–117
traffic violations, 123, 132
training, for investigators, 19–45
    benefits of, 25–26
    and college graduates, 16

training, for investigators *Continued*
  in financial matters, 26–29
  and in-house security, 21–26
  lack of, 21
  model program for, 22–25
  on-the-job, 16
  and private agencies, 19–21
training program model, 22–25
  materials used, 23–24
  objective of, 22
  schedule, 23–25
truck tails, 124
turnover, rate of, 20

Undercover (Motto), 65
undercover investigation
  agencies specializing in, 7
  in business/industry, 5–10
  history of, 1–10
  in law enforcement, 2–3
  limiting outside knowledge of, 50
  military/federal agencies, 3–5
  realistic expectations for, 63–64
underworld, the, infiltrating, 61–62

unions, 50–51
United States Army
  G-2 Section, Office of Special
    Investigations (OSI), 3
United States Treasury Balance
  pools, 30. *See also* gambling
  evidence of, 33–34
United States v. Maddox, 93
United States v. Russel, 91

vehicles, surveillance
  equipment in, 122
  modifications on, 122–123
  multiple, 123–124
  and truck tails, 124
  vans, 133

Wackenhut Agency, 7
Weinberg, Mel, 4
Winfield Security Corporation, 22
women, as investigators, 54
Word Trade Center, bombing, 4
workers' compensation, 27